A
Compounding
Life

A
Compounding
Life

*Lessons in Long-Term Thinking
from a Leading Endowment*

Ted Karns

DAMN GRAVITY

Published by Damn Gravity Media LLC, Chicago
www.damngravity.com

Cover photography by Craig Cole
Cover and interior design by Bookery

ISBNs
Hardcover: 978-1-962339-19-3
Paperback: 978-1-962339-21-6
Ebook: 978-1-962339-22-3
Audiobook: 978-1-962339-23-0

Printed in The United States of America

For Liz, Matthew, and Julia, with love and gratitude

Table of Contents

AUTHOR'S NOTE   ix

PRIMER *for the Curious Reader*   xi

INTRODUCTION   xiii

PART I: *Compounding Character*   1

CHAPTER 1: *Call Holding on Line 2:*
Career Transitions Are Built, Not Leapt   5

CHAPTER 2: *What Compounds First:*
Learning Resilience and Perspective   21

CHAPTER 3: *The Memo That Missed:*
Playing It Safe Is the Riskiest Move   37

CHAPTER 4: *From Boardroom to Blackboard:*
Humility and the Long View   49

PART II: *Compounding Capital*   61

CHAPTER 5: *The One for Sale:*
Reframing Risk, Earning Trust   65

CHAPTER 6: *Fewer, Better, Stronger:*
Building Real Partnerships   77

CHAPTER 7: *Building Conviction:*
Permission, Forgiveness, and Billion-Dollar Bets   87

CHAPTER 8: *Drawing the Line:*
When Partnership Means Saying No   99

CHAPTER 9: *Discipline in the Boom:*
Backing the Builders   111

PART III: *Compounding Relationships*   119

    CHAPTER 10: *Who Matters More Than When:*
    Avoiding Calendar Math   123

    CHAPTER 11: *Who Matters More Than What:*
    Investing in Friendship   131

    CHAPTER 12: *The Partnership Flywheel:*
    Learning Together over Chicken Parm   141

PART IV: *Compounding Purpose*   151

    CHAPTER 13: *Invest Well to Do Good:*
    Balancing Market Value and Your Values   155

    CHAPTER 14: *Persistence, Steadiness, Courage, Presence:*
    Finding Purpose in the People Who Shape Us   167

    CHAPTER 15: *The Long Arc of Purpose:*
    How Endowments Compound Opportunity   185

CONCLUSION *and an Invitation*   197

AFTERWORD: *The Identity Reinvention Project*   209

ACKNOWLEDGEMENTS   221

ABOUT *the Author*   225

Author's Note

This book is based on my personal experience over many years working in and around institutional investing. In Princeton, yes, but also in Hartford, Philadelphia, the Bay Area, Boston, and other places I've lived and worked.

To protect confidentiality and to focus on the broader lessons rather than specific people or organizations, I have changed some names, altered certain details, compressed timelines, and, in some cases, combined experiences. Dialogue is reconstructed from memory and reflects the substance rather than the precise wording of conversations. (I'm certain I've made myself sound more articulate than I actually was.)

To the extent that the stories are real, much of what I reference has already been shared publicly by former colleagues through interviews, articles, podcasts, and press releases. I've aimed to build on that foundation by focusing on broader lessons rather than institutional or individual specifics.

Some chapters—for example, those involving secondaries—are clearly amalgamations of multiple experiences across my career. They are not meant to portray any one person, event, or firm (even if I assign a name for storytelling purposes), but rather to reflect broader dynamics I encountered repeatedly in that part of the market. Similarly, figures such as the CIO are drawn from a blend of individuals I've worked with or observed over time. They are intended to reflect leadership dynamics and styles I've encountered across the industry, not any one person.

Nothing in this book should be taken as the view of any institution or person I have been or am currently affiliated with, including Princeton University, Boston University, Lincoln Financial Group, Bingham McCutchen, or any other organization. The views are entirely my own. The reflections, conclusions, and occasional exaggerations are also my own.

This book is not intended to offer or substitute for professional advice. It contains no investment, legal, tax, or other financial advice and should not be relied upon as such. (In other words, don't blame me if your crypto investment goes wrong.) Past performance mentioned, if any, is purely illustrative, and readers should consult qualified professionals before making any financial, career, or investment decisions. (And, yes, you can probably tell at this point that I did attend law school.)

This entire book is meant to be educational and informational. My aim is to share ideas and experiences that I hope will be useful to others navigating the world of long-term investing, leadership, career decision-making, and simply living a life aligned with your values.

I've written this with the intention of honoring the spirit of the work, the lessons learned, and the people and institutions that shaped my journey. Some recollections, especially those from decades ago, reflect how I remember them—not necessarily how others experienced them. Where memory may differ from fact, the fault is entirely mine.

Primer for the Curious Reader

For those not steeped in endowments,
private equity, or investing terms and acronyms.

If you're not from the world of endowments or private investing, don't worry. This book isn't written for insiders. However, a few quick definitions might help provide context for what follows.

Endowments are long-term pools of capital held by institutions like universities, hospital systems, and foundations. They invest that capital to support their missions into perpetuity, in effect providing intergenerational equity. The **endowment model** refers to a long-term, relationship-driven investment approach built on diversification, discipline, and patience. I spent much of my career at Princeton University's endowment. The university office charged with managing that endowment is the Princeton University Investment Company, or **Princo** for short.

In the private markets, **limited partners** (**LPs**) are institutions, such as endowments, that commit capital to funds, and **general partners** (**GPs**) are the investment managers running those funds. I sometimes refer to GPs as managers or firms, and LPs as allocators. LPs provide the capital; GPs put it to work by selecting investments, building portfolios, and managing exits.

Private equity (**PE**) and **venture capital** (**VC**) involve investing in companies that aren't publicly traded. These are long-term investments—often ten years or more—so trust, alignment, and judgment matter deeply.

When LPs invest in a fund, they make a **commitment**—a pledge to provide capital that's drawn down gradually over time. These commitments are typically funded in stages as opportunities arise.

CIO stands for **chief investment officer**, the person leading an institution's overall portfolio and investment team. A **managing director** (**MD**) is a senior investor, often leading an asset class like private equity and/or venture capital. MDs help shape strategy, build manager relationships, and guide long-term outcomes.

You may also see terms like **secondaries**, which involve buying or selling fund interests before they have naturally matured, and **carry**, short for **carried interest**, which is the GP's share of profits if things go well. GPs also charge LPs a **management fee** in addition to the carry.

No need to memorize any of this. There won't be a quiz. (Unless you happen to end up in one of my intro to finance classes, in which case, there might be a quiz. But I promise it won't be on secondaries.)

Introduction

He came to office hours full of energy. A freshman at Boston University, clearly smart, engaged, and serious about building a career in finance. He told me, almost breathlessly, that he'd joined every finance-related club on campus: the investment club, the consulting club, a fintech initiative, even the venture capital (VC) club. And now, he wanted to start one of his own, the investment banking club.

It was impressive. Also, a little exhausting just listening to it.

As he talked, it became clear that he wasn't just trying to learn; he was trying to do everything. Keep every option open. Signal ambition in all directions. I could see where this was going. He was going to stretch himself too thin, dilute his energy, and miss the real opportunities that come from actually going deep on something.

I probably should have just nodded and said, "Sounds great, good luck." But this pattern was familiar to me, and I soon found myself giving advice he probably didn't want to hear.

I told him what I've come to believe is one of the most important lessons in both investing and in life: Depth compounds more than breadth.

I encouraged him to slow down. Pick one or two communities where he could build meaningful relationships. Spend time getting to know the faculty sponsor of his favorite club. Stop collecting lines on a résumé and start building trust, credibility, and connection. The kind of things that don't show up immediately but grow quietly over time.

He nodded politely. I suspect he ignored most of what I said and kept joining clubs anyway. That's probably what I would have done at eighteen.

That conversation stayed with me, because it reflected something I've seen again and again, not just in students, but in professionals, investors... even in myself. This instinct to do more, reach farther, chase everything. Stay busy. The more-is-better approach that feels like progress but often isn't.

In my experience, it is intention—purposeful, focused action—that compounds rather than just activity. Being thoughtful and deliberate may look slower, but it builds more over time. It's not how many things I touched, but how deeply I engaged with the ones that mattered.

I have also found that quieter qualities don't appear all at once: Persistence is built over time, presence changes relationships, courage opens new doors, and purpose steadies the long arc of life. These qualities grow out of small decisions, made consistently and with care, until one day they amount to something much larger than you could have imagined.

This book evolved from reflections like this. Drawn from investing, teaching, mentoring, living, and simply trying to figure things out as I went along.

I spent fifteen years managing Princeton University's private equity and venture capital portfolio, working with people who were much smarter than I was about finance and markets, and much more skilled at Excel. Later, I started teaching finance to undergraduates, some of whom knew more about discounted cash flow models than I expected, and some of whom audibly gasped when I demonstrated the power of compounding in their future retirement accounts. And, I've been fortunate to learn from demanding bosses, patient teachers, and generous peers who shaped my path more than they know.

Somewhere along the way, I started writing. At first, those reflections became short essays—things I wrote simply because I needed to make sense of what I was learning. But over time, patterns emerged. I found that my writing was clarifying my own thinking.

Eventually, I wrote to share these thoughts with students, early-career professionals, my children—whose curiosity and resilience continue to make me proud—and with anyone else who seemed interested in how things actually work versus how they're supposed to work. I wanted to share that early failures aren't permanent, and that progress often looks quieter and messier than people admit.

This isn't a book about getting everything right. It's about learning through mistakes (I certainly made a lot), earning trust slowly, and realizing that meaningful work rarely feels like success while you're doing it. If these stories help someone feel a little less alone in that process, then writing them down was worth it.

Each chapter stands on its own. You don't have to read them in order, though there's a loose progression from character to capital to relationships to purpose. In addition, each chapter ends with two reflections that carry the story forward. In the reflection, "What Compounds," I look at the habits, relationships, and ideas that quietly built momentum over time. In "What Endures," I share the lessons that lasted—and, in some cases, an update on how those lessons still shape my work and life today. These sections aren't meant as summaries, but as invitations to pause and reflect, to see how the forces of compounding play out in the moment, as well as across years and even decades.

You'll also notice that certain themes surface again and again in these sections. That's not an accident. The lessons of compounding—whether in character, capital, relationships, or purpose—echo across different parts of life and career. Each story has its own texture and takeaways, but the overlaps are what give compounding its strength. The chapters, all together, offer a long-term lens for work, leadership, learning, and life.

And perhaps more importantly, they offer a countercultural way of thinking.

The dominant voices in our culture today rarely talk about compounding. They talk about disruption. About chasing alpha. About overnight success, immediate traction, how to "scale quickly" and "fail fast." We glorify what appear to be overnight wins and overlook the years of toil behind them. But the work that matters most rarely trends. It doesn't spike. It compounds. Most meaningful growth, in my experience, doesn't come from a flash of insight or a lucky break. It comes from small, deliberate steps repeated over time, often without recognition or applause.

Some might hear the word *compounding* and think of the literal act of combining two things. I mean it in the sense we use it in finance: earning interest on interest, where the returns themselves generate even more returns, creating exponential growth. As the saying about compound interest (often attributed to Princetonian Albert Einstein) goes, "Those who understand it, earn it; those who don't, pay it."

The saying is referring to money, but it's just as true in life. The same force that makes a small investment grow can make a small problem swell into something overwhelming if left unattended. Compounding works both ways—for you and against you. I've experienced both—times when it propelled me forward, and times when it dragged me under. In these pages, I share how compounding accelerated my progress, and how I learned to harness it in character, capital, relationships, and purpose so it worked in my favor, day after day, year after year.

This is a book for anyone questioning the rush. For those who feel the pressure to go viral or constantly pivot, but sense there is a better way. It's for people who want to build things that last: relationships, careers, reputations, families. It's about choosing to focus instead of flailing. About choosing depth instead of distraction.

And yes, it's also about investing. But maybe not the kind of investing people usually write books about. It's not a strategy guide. There are no performance charts or due diligence checklists. But there is a kind of investing that shapes the lives we lead, and not just the funds we manage: investing in people, ideas, and the long-term view.

That's where my experience with one of the largest university endowments in the world comes in. An endowment is a permanent pool of capital—typically at a university or foundation—invested to support a mission for decades, or even centuries. It's easy to miss just how much of our society's progress depends on institutions that are built to think long-term. Endowments are institutional investors, yes. But they're also engines of access and innovation.

Endowments have made quality education more affordable, launched generations of scholars and entrepreneurs, and quietly underwritten the research behind countless breakthroughs. If you trace the funding behind a Nobel Prize discovery or a breakthrough in pediatric cancer research, there's a good chance you'll find an endowment at the root of it. If a first-generation college student finds a fully funded path to college, there is likely an endowment at work. In a world obsessed with immediacy, endowments are one of the few places where the investment horizon still stretches for decades; where patience isn't a liability, but a strategy.

Endowments are more than just the setting for many of the stories that follow. They shaped my career and much of what I learned about investing, leadership, and patience. I also believe that endowment principles—thinking long-term, compounding small advantages, balancing risk with potential return—apply to life and career just as much as they do to finance.

And yet, most people have little idea of how they actually work. This book offers a window into the endowment mindset—the way decisions are made, the values that matter, the tradeoffs that define success over decades rather than quarters. And I'll admit, I do want to defend them. They are among the most powerful engines of access, opportunity, and innovation in our world.

I wrote this for anyone trying to build something meaningful over the long term. Whether you're navigating your first job or your fifth; whether you're managing someone else's money or trying to figure out what to do with your own; whether you're teaching others or still learning what matters most.

Because over time, it's not just your investments that compound. Everything does, if you let it.

PART I

Compounding Character

CHARACTER IS RARELY FORMED by a single dramatic event, nor revealed through one extraordinary act. Rather, character quietly accumulates over time. It is shaped through small choices, steady actions, and subtle responses to challenges, setbacks, and opportunities. Like financial compounding, the true power of character becomes evident across decades.

In my life and career, I've seen how character forms the foundation upon which everything else rests: professional growth, relationships (personal and career), leadership, and ultimately, meaningful impact. It emerges gradually, strengthened through persistence, integrity, humility, and curiosity. It's particularly revealed when circumstances become difficult, uncertain, or uncomfortable.

Another way character shows up is in how we treat one another in small moments. I saw this vividly at Princeton's endowment, where even the structure of our investment meetings reflected the values we hoped to live by. In our bull-bear meetings—the decision meetings for new investments—every team member would cast a vote, but the discussion always began with the most junior person in the room, even if it was an intern on his or her first day. That was our process. By starting with the individual with the least powerful voice, we reminded ourselves that everyone's perspective had value. Over time, this process compounded into confidence for junior team members, accountability for those more senior, and trust across the entire team. That's character at work—built in the quiet habits of listening and respect.

My path hasn't been linear or predictable. I've learned far more from my missteps, challenges, and unexpected turns and twists than from any quick success. Each experience, positive or negative, was another small contribution to character. Those contributions shaped my understanding of resilience, self-awareness, trust, and patience. They are the intangible assets that matter deeply in any meaningful endeavor.

Of course, some of those early lessons came with a healthy dose of humility. Like the time I was working around the clock at my law firm in Hartford, Connecticut, so sleep deprived that I called our IT helpline, convinced my BlackBerry was buzzing louder and louder. The tech support woman listened patiently to my increasingly frantic description before gently suggesting that, as long as it wasn't talking to me yet, I should probably just go home and get some sleep. Not my finest moment of professional composure. Moments like that reminded me that humility isn't just a nice quality—it's often the first step toward growth.

In my mind, before we can compound capital or relationships, we first must compound the foundation beneath it all. Part 1 explores how character compounds through different kinds of challenges:

career transitions built through small steps, resilience learned through early adversity, and the courage to take the right kinds of risks when it matters most. Whether you realize it or not, character is always compounding—sometimes quietly, sometimes painfully—and shaping the trajectory of a life and career.

CHAPTER 1

Call Holding on Line 2:
Career Transitions Are Built, Not Leapt

I WAS AT MY DESK, early 2004, trapped on the phone with a perfectly nice man who was about to offer me a perfectly reasonable job that would slowly bore me to death.

He was the general counsel at a small insurance company, one of my law firm's clients, walking me through the benefits package and company culture of their legal department. Safe work. Steady hours. A major improvement in lifestyle from law firm life. The kind of job that made sense on paper, especially with a young family.

But as he talked, all I could think was: I would be doing the same thing every day for the next twenty years.

That's when my Line 2 rang.

I used it as an excuse to pause the conversation. "Can I call you back in a few minutes?" I asked, probably with more relief in my voice than was polite.

It was Brad, the head of private investments at Lincoln Financial Group, one of my favorite clients. Brad was friendly as always.

"Ted," he said, "would you consider coming to Lincoln? Not directly onto my investment team, but through the general counsel's office. You'd be supporting our private investments from the legal side."

I couldn't believe that, after months of fantasizing about getting out of my firm, and having absolutely no time to look for a new job, I was now facing potentially two job offers.

Years later, through dozens of lectures at places like Princeton University, Harvard Business School, and Boston University, I've seen a pattern. Almost every time I share my background with students, a hand goes up, and someone asks, "How did you make the transition from law to investing?" It's often because it appears that I made a sharp pivot from practicing law to managing private equity and venture capital for one of the world's leading endowments. However, the reality is far less straightforward or dramatic. My path wasn't a single leap. It was a gradual evolution, built through small, deliberate steps, along with strong relationships, persistence, and plenty of luck.

I grew up on the South Shore of Boston, affectionately called the Irish Riviera. My childhood wasn't easy; my father died of cancer when I was eight, and my siblings and I escaped a house fire when I was ten. As you would expect, those experiences deeply impacted me and my family, but they also taught me about resilience, persistence, and navigating adversity. More on this part of my life in the next chapter.

Growing up in a traditional Irish-American Catholic family, the ultimate career roles were clear: lawyer, doctor, priest, or disappointment to your mother. I wasn't cut out for medicine or the priesthood, so law felt like the natural path if I wanted to be truly "successful" and avoid disappointing my mother.

That said, I certainly wasn't a model student early on. In high school and college, my academic record was inconsistent—strong at times, but uneven, depending on what else was going on in my life. It wasn't until law school that I really found my stride. I approached it differently, with more discipline and purpose, and ended up graduating with the highest GPA in my class. That experience taught me an early and lasting lesson: Success isn't about innate talent—it's more driven by persistence, preparation, and seizing the moment.

After law school, I joined Bingham McCutchen, a large Boston-based firm, in their institutional finance group in Hartford. The hours were long, but the work gave me something invaluable: early exposure to how sophisticated institutional investors structured their private investments. I wasn't making investment decisions, as I was focused on helping structure and document them. However, through this work, I began to understand how investors thought about risk, opportunity, and relationships. I didn't realize it at the time, but I was starting to build the foundation for a future career beyond law.

I was also fortunate to work closely with Jim, a senior partner at Bingham who became an important mentor. Jim taught me the technical skills I needed to draft and negotiate complex legal agreements, but more importantly, he showed me what it meant to build strong, trusted relationships with clients. Watching him work, I saw firsthand that technical excellence matters, but so does credibility, empathy, and reliability. Those early lessons about trust and client service stayed with me long after I left law practice.

Back to the call on Line 2.

By 2004, after three years at Bingham, I knew I needed to make a change. I was working eighty hours per week, and law firm life was burning me out, while my wife, Liz, and I were building a family. I was desperate for a different path that would allow me to have both a fulfilling career and the kind of family life we wanted together.

That's how I ended up on that call with the boring insurance company. Safe harbor from law firm life, but something about it felt like a trap.

When Brad called, he wasn't just offering me another legal job. He was offering me proximity to the investment world I'd been watching from the legal sidelines. If I accepted the job at Lincoln, I would serve as their in-house lawyer but would also sit in on investment team meetings. Importantly, Brad himself had started his career as a lawyer before moving into investing, and he understood the transition I might someday want to make. Later, when I expressed an interest in shifting toward investing, Brad and another senior executive, Rich, gave me my first real shot at an investment role. I'm forever grateful.

Of course, when I got the offer from Lincoln's legal department, there were serious tradeoffs to consider. Accepting would mean relocating my family from Connecticut to the Philadelphia area—much further from Boston and my extended family. Housing in the Philly suburbs was also more expensive than in Hartford, made more acute by the new role's modest pay cut.

But that phone call opened a new door, and I walked through it, taking the offer. If Brad hadn't reached out at that moment, I might have accepted the other job that would have led me down a very different, more stagnant path. Luck played a role, but so did preparation, persistence, and building trusted relationships (that is, Brad called me rather than the associate in the next office).

At Lincoln, I made it a point not just to handle the legal work, but to learn everything I could about the investments themselves. I asked questions constantly. I sat in on investment committee meetings. I listened more than I spoke.

At the same time, I began studying for the Chartered Financial Analyst (CFA) Level I exam—the first step toward a professional investing credential—to deepen my technical understanding of finance and investing. I knew that if I wanted to make a serious transition into investing, I had to prepare in ways that weren't strictly required by my current role.

In 2006, after about eighteen months supporting the private investments team as counsel, I formally transitioned into an investing role. And, there's no way I could have made that shift on my own. Brad and Rich gave me the chance, and then patiently taught me how to think like an investor. Jayson, a brilliant peer, pushed me every day with his insight and rigor. The three of them shaped my early education in investing more than any class or exam ever could. It wasn't glamorous at first—lots of Excel (which was new to me), memos, diligence work, and analysis—but I was investing. And I loved it.

In January 2008, everything shifted again. Lincoln's new CEO decided to suspend the private equity investment program indefinitely. I could have stayed to manage the existing portfolio, but I knew I wanted to be somewhere where private equity wasn't an extracurricular; it was the core mission.

Rather than wait for job openings, I decided to be proactive. Among others, I cold-emailed Andy, the chief investment officer (CIO) at Princeton University Investment Company (Princo), the office that managed the university's endowment. But I didn't ask for a job. I introduced myself, shared my background, and said I would love the opportunity to connect and learn. I expressed admiration for Princo's long-term investment philosophy and told him, honestly, that I had a lot to learn.

Around the same time, I wrote a similar email to Narv, Columbia University's CIO at the time, who would later go on to lead Harvard's endowment. He was quite generous with his time and gave me valuable advice on the endowment world that proved helpful when I later talked to Andy. Narv didn't have an open position at the time, but he continued to be a trusted mentor for years. I'm grateful, and I have admired the challenging work he has done at Harvard, moving an endowment culture that historically leaned short-term into one with a long-term orientation.

That distinction of seeking to learn rather than claiming I could "add value from day one" when I first reached out to Andy turned out to be crucial. Later, when I helped hire analysts at Princo, I saw how off-putting it can be when candidates without experience insist they can contribute immediately at an institution with a top track record. Humility, curiosity, and a genuine desire to grow are much better foundations. Over the years, I noticed that those who arrived with less bravado often advanced more quickly, because they listened, adapted, and earned credibility step by step. For me, that stance created room to absorb more, to admit what I didn't know, and to make mistakes without pretense. It built trust faster than forced confidence ever could, and that trust made the Princo team eager to invest in my growth.

Fortunately, Andy responded to my email as well. He and his fellow senior leader, Jon, agreed to meet. And eventually, Princo decided to take a chance on me, not because I was fully formed (in fact, that would have been a negative), but because I was willing to learn.

As I was weighing this opportunity at Princeton, I called one of my most trusted mentors, Mark. He was a family friend of Liz's, not someone I grew up with—no one in my world back then was in PE. Mark had retired early after a remarkable career as one of the pioneers in the field, arranging some of the largest and most innovative PE financings of his time. He listened carefully, then reminded me to think less about the title and more about the kind of learning and community I wanted around me. That conversation helped me recognize Princeton as more than a job change—it was a chance to grow alongside some of the world's very best investors.

Still, the offer gave me pause. The job title was clearly below the one I held at Lincoln, and it felt like a step back. When I joined Lincoln, it was with a modest pay cut, which strangely felt easier than this downgrade in title. Only I knew my compensation, but everyone could see my title. That felt humbling.

Andy told me he was doing it intentionally—so I'd feel free to ask the dumb questions. He didn't want me arriving with something to prove, but with space to learn and grow faster than I otherwise might have. At the time, though, I was a little stung by it. So, I asked for more money than he'd offered—compensation that, frankly, was already a meaningful step up from Lincoln. Andy was clearly annoyed, but he did come back with more. It felt like a small victory to me in the back-and-forth over the title.

At the time, it felt like friction; in hindsight, it was propulsion. The lower title gave me the freedom to ask the dumb questions, and the small victory on compensation boosted my confidence. Asking for more money may not have been my wisest decision, but it did teach me that confidence and humility can coexist—and sometimes need to.

Princo was a step into a new culture of excellence. When I joined in 2008, Princo had one of the strongest investment track records in the world and was the envy of the institutional investing field. The endowment had outstanding performance by any measure, and I was about to join the team that accomplished this.

Getting the chance to join Princo felt surreal—as if I'd been called up to the Red Sox, stepping into a clubhouse of champions where the bar was impossibly high. And not just the Red Sox, but the Red Sox right after their 2007 World Series championship. Simply earning a spot felt like a win, and also like the start of a new kind of pressure.

When I started, of course, I wasn't leading anything. I spent my early days learning, contributing, and growing within a team that expected rigor, humility, teamwork, and constant improvement.

Despite my enthusiasm, my first year at Princo was tough. The global financial crisis hit shortly after I started. Markets were collapsing, and the institution faced real pressure. Not being a Princeton alumnus, I couldn't help feeling like an outsider. And, outside work, moving my family to Princeton, a town very different from where we had lived before, was hard.

And then I made matters worse.

I had focused heavily on performing well individually. I built strong relationships with the senior team and spent significant time mentoring and developing younger colleagues. But what I missed, at least initially, was the importance of peer relationships. At Princo, success wasn't just about standing out individually. It was about being competitive as a team—raising the performance of the entire group, not just yourself. This was quite a different culture than a 1,000-attorney global law firm, which was ultra-competitive on an individual basis. We even had a leaderboard that ranked associate attorneys on their total billable hours. In my first year at the law firm, I finished at the top of my cohort. Not something I'm proud of now. At Princo, the only leaderboard that mattered was the collective one—how we performed as a team.

At the end of my first year, a promotion I was in line for was delayed. It stung, but the reason for the delay was also the best feedback I could have received. I needed to invest more energy in building trust, collaboration, and partnership with my direct peers, not just up and down the organization.

I took that lesson seriously. I worked hard to strengthen internal relationships at every level. I communicated with my colleagues more fully, listened better, and thought constantly about how my work fit into the team's success. Six months later, I earned the promotion. Four years after joining, I was promoted to managing director, co-leading the private equity and venture capital portfolio, one of the largest and most important allocations in Princeton's endowment—indeed, the endowment's compounding engine.

And perhaps even more meaningfully, the peer who was a key part of that early feedback and I both went on to build amazing careers, supporting each other at every turn, and we remain friends to this day, seventeen years later. We just had lunch together in Boston when she was in town for an annual meeting. The lesson I learned about valuing relationships over competition has been instrumental in shaping my career.

One final lesson that stands out when I reflect on my career path: You don't have to make every hard decision alone.

At several pivotal moments, such as moving in-house to Lincoln, stepping toward investing, reaching out to Princo, and staying resilient during tough early years, I had someone I could talk to, someone I trusted completely. For me, that person is my wife. She has been my strategic advisor, sounding board, strongest supporter, and biggest fan. Liz has a rare way of getting to the heart of things with warmth and clarity. When I was struggling with doubt or overthinking the risks, she gently reminded me what mattered most. And when I hesitated, she believed in me more than I believed in myself. (Liz's most recent role has been a valued and trusted editor of this book.)

We've always approached decisions as partners—across all aspects of life. Her support has been about thinking things through together, asking each other the right questions, and keeping sight of the bigger picture. She's helped me remember that career decisions are more than new titles or outcomes—they're about building a life we both believe in and can be proud of.

However, the lesson is not that one needs a spouse to be successful. That person could be a mentor, a sibling, a parent, or a close friend. Having someone outside of your professional world, someone who knows you deeply, believes in you, and can give honest feedback and encouragement, makes a huge difference. For me, that is Liz.

Just as in investing, where we often prefer backing teams over solo founders, having a partner you trust—someone to challenge you, steady you, and push you to think longer-term—can be one of the most important factors in building a meaningful, resilient career.

What Compounds

Career transitions usually aren't grand moves. They are built slowly, by staying curious, building relationships, preparing quietly, and being ready to act when the moment arrives.

Many of my own pivots came earlier than I felt ready for, which taught me an important lesson: It's okay, even wise, to move before you feel fully ready. Preparation isn't about eliminating uncertainty; it's about building a strong enough foundation to walk through the next open door with confidence and humility.

Another lesson: Transitions don't always look like transitions at first. Sometimes they're disguised as a side project, a new seat in the same room, or a call from someone who sees your potential before you do. Sometimes the pivot comes not from a grand vision, but from a glimpse—a moment of clarity that one path might just lead somewhere better than the one you're on. Of course, not every career unfolds this way. Some people do make bold leaps into entirely new fields, and for the right person at the right time, that can work beautifully. For me, it was smaller, steadier steps that proved the right path.

Through these small steps, certain qualities began to compound. Curiosity compounded. Every question I asked in a meeting, every extra hour I spent learning Excel or prepping for CFA Level 1, every conversation where I listened more than I spoke... those all layered into something valuable: I slowly learned to think like an investor. Credibility compounded, too. From law firm deals to in-house diligence to endowment decision-making, each role built trust. I didn't have to sell myself for the next job because people already had a sense of how I worked and who I was.

Relationships open more doors than résumés. Brad called me not because I had perfect credentials (indeed, I doubt he had ever seen my résumé at that point), but because I had earned trust and credibility. And I kept building that trust over time with mentors, peers, teammates, and eventually, the people I helped recruit and coach. Those relationships compounded over time, shaping how I think, how I work, and how I lead.

One thing I didn't anticipate compounding was a quiet habit: responding to people who reach out, especially those brave enough to reach out cold. Students, recent grads, mid-career professionals unsure what's next... I try to make time. Because I remember being in their shoes—writing to people like Narv and Andy, unsure if anyone would reply. And I remember how much those conversations shaped what came next. What started as a single thoughtful response has grown into a rhythm, a practice. Over time, it's built trust, relationships, and a sense of continuity. The chance to help someone else the way others helped me—often without knowing how much it mattered.

Excellence is not just about performance. It's about growth and continual learning. It's about how you show up, how you improve, how you react to setbacks. Promotions, transitions, and new chapters often follow periods of friction and recalibration. In fact, my best growth came after my hardest feedback and setbacks. That humility also compounded. I didn't show up at Princo trying to impress everyone. I showed up ready to learn. It made me coachable, open to feedback, and willing to see the bigger picture. Over time, that humility made me a better teammate and, eventually, a better leader and mentor.

And perhaps most unexpectedly: Mission compounded, too. I didn't start the Princeton journey because I wanted to serve an institution's mission. I started because I wanted to learn from the best. But over time, I saw how great investing could fund great opportunities—for students, faculty, even entire fields of study. That deeper purpose changed the way I thought about capital, risk, and impact.

What Endures

After fifteen years at Princeton, I decided in 2023 to leave Princo, fully moving back to the South Shore of Boston. This wasn't a sudden decision. I had first shared my plans with Princeton's leadership in late 2019 because I wanted to be open and fair with my senior colleagues and give them plenty of time to plan for the future. At that time, my plan was to leave in the summer of 2021, when our daughter would finish high school. Just as in every other stage of my career, I believed that trust and transparency mattered most.

When the time came, I was asked to stay longer than I originally planned, and I agreed to continue to work "remotely" to help ensure a smooth transition. Over time, though, the back-and-forth travel made it hard to fully settle back into life in Boston while also being fully present for my Princo colleagues, especially my junior team members. Eventually, I made the decision to step away and close that chapter.

Coming back to Boston's South Shore feels like coming full circle. In my experience, people from Boston either stay forever or spend their lives trying to get back, and I now understand why. To me, it's the greatest city in the world. Being part of the greater Boston community again has been a dream come true.

One of the gifts of returning has been the chance to turn more professional relationships into close friendships. Pat, a partner at a leading PE firm, has a house nearby, and that first summer, he invited me to go sailing. I hadn't been on a sailboat in decades—not since middle school, when my stepfather and I would take out the boat he had built himself. To be back on those same waters nearly forty years later was centering.

Pat has had tremendous success in his career, but you'd never know it from spending time with him. He's quick to laugh, generous with his time, and always looking for ways to help others. He has the Irish gift of gab—curious about your experiences, but just as ready to share his own with warmth and humor. Those afternoons reminded me that relationships, like careers, don't leap forward in a single moment. They build slowly, through time, trust, and shared experience.

I'm grateful for the growth, relationships, and experiences of my time at Princeton, and equally grateful to be back where my story began, building the next chapter. I'm also proud of the example I've been able to share with my children, who themselves continue to inspire me.

Sometimes I think about that phone call from Brad, interrupting what could have been a very different conversation about a very different future. Career transitions are built, not leapt—and sometimes they're built one phone call at a time.

If you're early in your career—or considering a change at any stage—and wondering how to find your own path forward, you don't need to have it all figured out. What matters is moving toward things that challenge and stretch you, trusting that those small steps will compound into something meaningful. That's how most real transitions happen, not with a five-year or ten-year plan and a clean story, but with a door you decide to walk through before you know exactly what's on the other side. Looking back, career growth really does feel like compounding: small, consistent efforts layered over time until they create exponential impact.

Your path doesn't need to look like anyone else's (certainly not like mine!), but if you stay engaged and keep learning and growing, it will take you somewhere that is meaningful to you.

CHAPTER 2

What Compounds First:
Learning Resilience and Perspective

WHEN I GIVE GUEST lectures to students about careers and investing, I'm often asked to share my professional path: how I moved from law to institutional investing, what I learned at Princeton's endowment, and how I think about career transitions.

I always start the same way: with my childhood, because that's where I learned what resilience really means.

Students sometimes look surprised. They're expecting to hear about why I went to law school, or networking strategies, or how to break into finance. Instead, I tell them about losing my father when I was eight and escaping a house fire when I was ten.

It's certainly not because I think everyone needs to experience tragedy to be successful in their careers. It's because I believe that how we learn to handle adversity early on shapes how we navigate everything that follows: the setbacks, the opportunities, and the moments when we have to choose between giving up and finding a way forward.

The truth is, most of us face significant challenges at some point in our lives. Some are visible, and you can see them just by looking at someone; others are completely hidden, and you have no idea what the person sitting next to you in a meeting or a classroom has been through (or is currently going through). We all learn from these experiences, and they shape how we approach everything else.

Your early experiences don't dictate where you'll end up or how successful you'll be. However, they do help determine how you respond when things don't go according to plan. And in any meaningful career, things never go completely according to plan.

So, when students ask me about resilience, about taking risks, about handling failure and rejection, I start at the beginning. Because that's where I first learned what resilience actually looks like, and that's where I developed the perspective that has helped me keep career challenges in their proper context.

When you've experienced real loss, the professional setbacks that feel devastating to others, like not getting the promotion, losing a deal, being passed over for an opportunity... yes, they might hurt, but they don't get even close to breaking you. You understand the difference between disappointment and tragedy. That perspective doesn't make you care less about your career; it helps you navigate it with clearer judgment about what's actually worth worrying about.

I used to only think about how good things compound in life. Success builds on success, opportunities create more opportunities, momentum carries you forward. That's the story we tell about careers and compound growth and building toward something better.

But that's not how it worked for me. For me, the challenges compounded first. For others, challenges come later; for some, they are ever-present.

My father got sick when I was six or seven. Cancer. I didn't understand what that meant at all, not really. In fact, I recall the first time someone told me he had cancer. It was on the playground, playing soccer. We were like a swarm of bees following the ball around the field. I think I knew that something was quite wrong at home, but no one had ever told me he had cancer until a classmate came up to me on that field and said, "Your dad has cancer." It seems like an odd thing to say, reflecting on it now, but six- and seven-year-olds just blurt out whatever is on their minds. I got quite angry until a friend came over and told me to ask my mom about it. The soccer game went on.

I understood the trips to Boston for surgeries, the countless weekends at my Nana's house in Dorchester while my parents were unavailable, the gradual sense that something was very wrong in our house. But no one ever explicitly told me what was actually happening until I confronted my mom about it when I got home from school that day.

Dorchester, one of Boston's largest and most diverse neighborhoods, where my father grew up, was different from our quiet suburban neighborhood in Norwell. Kids were tougher there, even at that age. They grew up faster. I absorbed some of that during those weekend stays—a different kind of education about how to handle yourself and how to be resilient when things don't go your way. So, I was growing up faster than most at home, but also in a different way on the weekends.

By the time my father died when I was eight, I'd already learned that life doesn't follow the script that you expect it to.

I remember lying in bed asking the question every kid asks when something terrible happens: Why me? Why did my dad have to die? How did I get so unlucky?

Then I'd feel terrible for thinking that. Because I didn't die. He did. He was only thirty-six. His life got cut short, not mine. I was still here; I still had a chance at everything he wouldn't get to see.

That guilt about feeling sorry for myself was probably my first real lesson in perspective. Understanding that my pain was real, but so was everyone else's. And sometimes other people's pain is much, much bigger than your own.

It's a hard lesson for an eight-year-old. It stuck.

What I remember most about the months after my father died wasn't my own grief. It was watching my mother try to figure out how to keep our family together and moving forward.

She was thirty-four years old with three kids: my sister, who was ten, me at eight, and my brother, who was five. My father hadn't left much life insurance. She had no real career to fall back on. And she was dealing with her own grief while trying to manage ours. Unfortunately, as a family, we dealt with grief by mostly ignoring it. By not talking about my father. Almost never.

I didn't quite understand it then, but looking back, she was clearly grieving. She would spend hours just sitting in the living room. If I wanted to find her, she was likely just sitting there with her eyes closed. "Resting her eyes," she would say.

Home had been our constant since my father died. It seemed like a safe place. He had died in our house, and all our memories were there. It was small: three bedrooms, one full bath, with a little addition off the kitchen that we used as a family room. Our first floor was heated by a coal stove. All winter, my brother and I carried in buckets of coal and hauled the hot ashes out to the woods behind the house. It felt old-fashioned even then, but it was just part of life—the same woods that took our ashes also held our forts and adventures beyond the back door.

But even that constant was about to come under attack.

It was a typical Sunday night, two years after my father died. My mom had gone out to a support group, leaving the three of us home alone. My brother and I were lying on the floor of the family room watching the Muppets. My sister was in the kitchen trying to make us something for dinner. We were still only twelve, ten, and seven.

I can't remember a night where we sat down for a family dinner after my dad died. We often just grabbed whatever was available, and that dark night, my sister was trying to get some food ready for her little brothers while my mom was out. Reflecting on it now and recognizing that it was a different time, that was too much to ask of a twelve-year-old.

The Muppet Show was just wrapping up, and suddenly I smelled smoke. My brother and I popped up from the floor, and we were literally standing in smoke. We ran toward the kitchen door. I saw the cabinets, the curtains over the sink, and the ceiling all engulfed in flames. The fire spread so fast. Since we were in the addition, there was a window into the kitchen, and I can still see the curtains on the other side of the window bursting into flames.

We stood in the doorway of the burning room and screamed for my sister. I screamed louder than I've ever screamed in my life. She suddenly appeared in the other entrance to the kitchen, on the other side of the burning room. I yelled for her to go out the front door and meet us in the front yard, but she was just standing there screaming—a blood-curdling scream of pure terror. I don't think she could hear me.

Then my sister started running toward us—right through the burning room, with flames on either side of her and on the ceiling. I can still see it in my mind. Thankfully, she reached us safely, and we all ran for the door.

"Run to the neighbors' house!" she yelled. "Get help!"

We ran full speed into the street and up their driveway. It seemed to take forever. My sister fell on the rock driveway about halfway to the house, and my brother and I quickly pulled her up. We kept running and screaming.

We made it to our neighbors' house and started banging on their kitchen door. Our neighbor came running across the kitchen and quickly opened the door. We somehow got out what had happened. Her husband said he would go see if he could put out the fire and ran toward our house. She called the fire department.

When my mom arrived and saw the fire engines, she ran toward the house, thinking we were inside. A firefighter practically tackled her as she was about to enter the burning building, and he told her we were at the neighbors' house. I don't remember her coming in, but I do remember my friend Jonathan's father showing up and sitting with us. He didn't say much, but his presence was comforting. Then, I recall feeling a massive sense of relief when my Uncle Roger walked through the door. It was remarkable how quickly people came. My other grandparents arrived later and took us all back to their condo in Plymouth for the night.

The house was severely damaged. The weight of the tragedies felt massive on us all.

But here's what I learned watching my mother in the weeks and months that followed: When everything falls apart, some people fall apart with it. But my mom found a way to build something new. It wasn't easy, and there certainly were tough moments. But she moved us forward.

She could have given up. She could have let the weight of losing her husband and then her home crush what was left of her spirit. Instead, she pushed forward.

We moved into a trailer for a year while the house was rebuilt. She took a job as an assistant for my father's cousin's business. She learned to handle everything: the insurance claims (both medical and fire), the decisions about where to live, and how to rebuild our lives.

I watched her do this day by day, decision by decision. I didn't understand at the time that I was getting a masterclass in resilience. I just knew that when everything seemed hopeless, she kept going.

In those months after we lost everything, help came from unexpected places. My Uncle Bud was a Holy Cross priest on mission in Peru, and his brothers in the order kept an eye on us. Father Bartley, the president of Stonehill College, regularly checked in on my mother, and Fathers Jim and Willy became reliable presences at family gatherings. These weren't grand gestures, just good deeds by a few priests who understood that sometimes families need people to show up. And, they were just three of many who helped us, including countless friends, neighbors, family members, and teachers.

I learned something important by watching my mother accept their help. She was fiercely independent, but she understood that refusing support wasn't strength; it was pride. Letting others help wasn't admitting defeat; it was building the relationships that would sustain us.

My Nana in Dorchester continued to be an important anchor. Many weekends, when my mother needed space to breathe, Nana would take us in. The routine never changed: The moment we walked through her door, she'd march me across the street to the neighbor's house, tell me to take off my shirt, and a nineteen-year-old girl training to be a hairdresser would cut my hair right there in her kitchen. As a late elementary school boy, a bit pudgy, sitting shirtless while a beautiful teenage girl cut my hair, it was mortifying.

Nana was a hard worker who'd saved every penny to buy her duplex in Dorchester. She was fiercely proud of it, loved her neighborhood of St. Brendan's, and was especially proud that my father, her only child, had made it to Boston College (on scholarship). Her own husband (my grandfather), a World War II veteran, had only finished grammar school. As one of eleven children raised by a widowed mother, he had to leave school to work and support the family. So, when my dad graduated from BC, it felt to Nana like the whole family had made it.

Now, she had lost her son and was often responsible for his three kids, weekend after weekend. But Nana just did what she'd always done: She took care of things. The haircuts weren't negotiable because her standards weren't negotiable. You showed up in the world looking like you mattered—clean cut—no matter what was happening at home.

———————

Sometimes, even in the hardest years, unexpected good things happen. The same year as the fire, an elementary school in our town closed, and about a third of those students joined our school. That's how I met my new best friend, Dave. He was super loyal, always supportive, and very outgoing. He and his father would let me hang out with them often. His dad did car repair out of their house for friends and family on weekends, and we'd drive around in his Chevy Nova going to auto parts stores, listening to the Irish music station. Growing up on the Irish Riviera (the South Shore of Boston), we actually had a radio station that just played Irish folk music.

To this day, Dave and I are good friends and see each other all the time. Dave actually became the fire chief in our hometown. He continues to be super loyal, always supportive, and very outgoing (read: *loud*, in a good way). And, I still listen to Irish music. Some of the best things in life come when you're not looking for them—often right when everything else is falling apart.

———————

Decades later, when I gave the eulogy at my mom's funeral, I talked about how she faced "numerous challenges throughout her life, from losing my dad with three young kids, to having a major house fire shortly thereafter, to developing Parkinson's at the age of fifty."

But what struck me as I was writing those words was what she became after all those challenges: someone who made everyone around her feel cared for. Someone who always had time to listen. Someone who could enter any room and make it feel more welcoming. And, my mom did this while Parkinson's shadowed her last two decades—a reminder that resilience isn't only forged in sudden loss, but also in the quiet courage of facing challenges every day.

She didn't just survive what happened to her. She transformed it into generosity.

The woman who spent hours sitting in the living room with her eyes closed after my father died became the woman who organized movie clubs and book clubs and quilling classes at the senior center. And, yes, I mean quilling, not quilting—quilling is an intricate paper art made from delicate rolled strips. She loved it, and over the years, she taught it to probably hundreds who might never have discovered it otherwise.

The woman who lost everything in a house fire became someone who always had her purse ready with origami paper and pop-up books and Kermit the Frog puppets to entertain any kid who needed it.

Her struggles and losses didn't disappear. But she found a way to build something beautiful on top of them.

What Compounds

Over the years, I came to realize what those experiences had left me with: the quiet building blocks of resilience and perspective. Resilience is not about falling down—it's about what you do when you get back up. Some of the most important lessons don't come from conversations or advice, but from watching other people handle impossible situations. My mother never sat me down and explained how to be resilient; she just showed me, day after day, what it looked like to keep going when everything seemed lost.

Perspective, too, is a gift that often comes wrapped in pain. As a child, I learned that life can change in an instant. Nothing is guaranteed. The people you love can be taken away. It was a hard lesson, but also the foundation for understanding what truly matters. I came to see that compound growth doesn't always start with advantages. Sometimes, it starts with challenges that force you to develop strength you didn't know you had.

When difficulties compound first, you build different muscles than you do from opportunities. You build endurance instead of confidence. Perspective instead of momentum. The ability to keep going when things get hard, instead of the expectation that things will keep getting easier. Those muscles served me throughout my career in ways I didn't recognize until much later. When I faced setbacks at Princeton—when deals fell through, when a promotion was delayed—I already knew what real loss felt like. I already understood that you can lose everything and still find a way forward.

The early losses also compounded into gratitude. When good things did start happening—getting into college, finding a spouse, landing jobs, having kids, building a career—I never took them for granted. I knew they could disappear, which made me appreciate them more and work harder to deserve them.

Looking back, I'm struck by how little we actually talked about what had happened. My father's illness. His death. The fire. It was like we had all agreed, silently, to carry it alone. I've come to believe that silence, while sometimes protective, can be its own kind of burden. To this day, I still struggle with that part—opening up and talking things through. I've gotten better, especially over the last several years. But frankly, it's still work. Real partnership and real leadership require vulnerability, and that hasn't always come naturally to me. I'm still learning.

But perhaps most importantly, watching my mother's resilience compounded into a deeper understanding of what strength actually looks like. It doesn't look like never falling down. It looks like falling down and getting back up and finding a way to help other people while you're doing it. That lesson shaped everything about how I approach challenges, relationships, and leadership. The best response to adversity isn't just personal recovery. It's being someone who helps others recover, too.

What Endures

What amazes me most, reflecting on those tough years, is how often my sister stepped up to take care of the family. She was only ten when my dad died and twelve at the time of the fire, but she became our anchor in ways no child should ever have to. Cooking for us. Watching us. Driving us everywhere, once she was old enough. Helping hold things together while all of us, including my mom, were still trying to make sense of the chaos. And I'm certain we never said thank you. Definitely not the way we should have. She was thrust into an impossible role—still only a child herself—and handled it with a strength that we all relied on without even realizing it. I'm extremely grateful.

The challenges that compounded first in my life weren't preparation for anything specific. They were just hard things that happened to our family.

But they built a foundation I've been standing on ever since. They taught me that resilience is real, that people can endure more than they think they can, and that sometimes the worst things that happen to you become the source of your greatest strengths. I've come to believe that's true for almost everyone: the hardest things we go through often build our inner resources—the quiet qualities of character—that carry us forward.

In writing this chapter, I've thought a lot about how character compounds not just in a person, but across generations.

My wife Liz has some of the same quiet strength my Nana had. The same instinct to take care of people without needing recognition. I didn't recognize it right away, but now I see it constantly.

People sometimes say we marry someone like our parents. I'm not sure that's quite true. I do, however, think we're drawn to character traits we recognize, especially the kind that shaped us early, before we could name them. Liz has that grounding presence my Nana had. That same quiet conviction. It's one of the things that has made her such a steady partner in my life—someone who brings out the best in me while holding our family steady.

It reminds me that character doesn't just grow. It gets passed on. It shows up in whom we choose to trust. With whom we build families. Who we become.

———————

A few years ago, hiking in remote Donegal, Ireland, with my family, I did something uncharacteristic: I sat down on a bench to rest. We'd passed ten other benches, but I never sit during hikes—I'm like the Energizer bunny. Liz started teasing me about taking a break until she suddenly went white as a ghost. The inscription on the bench I chose to sit on was a dedication to Father Bartley from Stonehill, from his hometown neighbors, celebrating the twenty-fifth anniversary of his ordination, proud that their local boy had become the president of an American college. I knew he was Irish (his brogue gave that away), but I didn't even realize he was from Donegal. Seriously, I'm not making this remarkable story up. I still can't believe it myself!

Father Bartley (like many, many others) had been part of our foundation when everything was falling apart. Thirty-five years later, in the remotest corner of his homeland, a few years after his death, I was literally resting on a monument to his life's work. Sometimes, the people who help build your character stay part of your story in ways you never expect.

———————

When students ask me about career transitions or taking risks or handling setbacks, I often think about those early lessons. Not because I think everyone needs to experience loss to be successful—certainly and hopefully not—but because I know that challenges are inevitable for everyone. You can learn from watching people handle them well.

Though my mother passed away a few years ago, her lesson remains: When everything falls apart, you have a choice. You can let it define you, or you can let it refine you.

She chose refinement. And in doing so, she showed me that sometimes what compounds first is character. And that foundation has carried me through everything that has come after.

CHAPTER 3

The Memo That Missed: Playing It Safe Is the Riskiest Move

C RUNCH.

There I was, a young law student driving my unimpressive red Ford Escort stick shift through downtown Hartford, with its glass towers and insurance company logos desperately trying to seem important—Britney Spears on the radio singing "Oops!... I Did It Again"—when I gently rear-ended someone at a set of lights on Whitney Avenue.

Not hard. Just a tap. I was shaking slightly as we exchanged insurance information. Not from the collision, as it was barely noticeable, but because I was already so tightly wound that even the smallest hiccup felt monumental.

Just fifteen minutes earlier, Liz and I had seen our first baby's heartbeat on an ultrasound, a tiny flicker on a grainy screen. Incredible, terrifying, and real. I was finishing law school, jobless, and was three weeks into a summer associate role at a Hartford law firm, where I'd already managed to mess up my first assignment.

The Ford Escort was red because nobody else wanted red. There were at least ten of them on the lot. It was the wrong color on the wrong car. But it was about all we could afford at the time. The salesman had even said, "I'm prepared to make you a very good deal on this car." On top of that, we'd stacked every possible discount: recent graduate, Ford credit card holder, summer promo, etc., until the salesman, visibly annoyed, finally surrendered. "You really can't combine all these," he kept saying. But we did. My father-in-law, who had a great sense of humor, called me a couple of days after we picked the car up, pretending to be someone from Ford, and said there had indeed been a mistake and we couldn't stack all the discounts. Embarrassingly, for a minute, I fell for it. We got such a good deal that a couple of years later, I sold that car for about what I paid for it new, which felt like a small victory after a summer full of defeats.

But at that moment, standing on the street in Hartford after my fender bender, holding my stomach like something fragile, I remember thinking, *I really can't afford another mistake.*

The pressure to perform perfectly is different for everyone. Perhaps it's to satisfy parents who sacrificed to pay for college. Maybe it's being the first in your family to get this kind of opportunity. Maybe it's just the crushing weight of your own expectations. But the feeling is the same: "I cannot afford to screw this up."

It started casually enough. A senior partner dropped a folder on my desk while breezing past: "Quick memo on Connecticut non-compete law. Due Thursday."

That was all. No guidance, no context, nothing about length or detail. Just the assignment.

I should have asked for clarity. How detailed? Who's the audience? What specifically do you need? But asking felt like admitting incompetence. Plus, he was already halfway down the hall, probably heading to another meeting, another crisis, another summer associate who hopefully wouldn't need their hand held.

So instead, I did exactly what any anxious, perfectionistic law student would do. I went deep. Really deep.

I stayed late three consecutive nights. I tracked down every case, every angle, every nuance, compiling a fifteen-page exhaustive analysis. I cited cases from the early 1900s. I included a footnote about Vermont law, just because it seemed relevant. I even found a law review article that mentioned non-competes in passing—a single line buried in eighty pages—because it seemed like the kind of thing a serious memo should include.

The partner thumbed through it for about thirty seconds. I watched him flip pages like he was looking for something that clearly wasn't there.

"This is way too broad. I don't have time to read all this. I just needed a quick memo on enforceability for tomorrow's client meeting. This reads like a law review article."

I felt a deep, sickening drop in my stomach.

"I can revise it..."

"Don't bother. I'll handle it."

Fifteen hours of work evaporated in a thirty-second skim. Not just off-target, completely irrelevant.

After that, I basically disappeared. In meetings, I'd sit quietly, listening while other summer associates jumped in. Some of their ideas were good, some weren't, but at least they were talking. I had ideas too, but I kept them buried. Better silent than wrong.

The conference room where this all played out was on the fifteenth floor, with windows facing the Connecticut River. The table was mahogany, or at least trying to be, with enough dings and coffee rings to tell stories about decades of deals gone right and wrong. The chairs were leather but cracked, the kind that made a little wheeze when you leaned back.

Mid-summer feedback was painfully direct:

"You're smart, you're hardworking, but we can't get a sense of who you are professionally."

Translation: You've vanished into the background.

I'd been thinking about risk completely backwards. Staying quiet felt safe, but it was actually guaranteeing failure—maybe not dramatic failure, but the slow fade of being forgettable. Speaking up might occasionally go wrong, but staying silent would definitely go nowhere.

I decided on a small new rule: Say one useful thing per day. Nothing earth-shattering. Just something relevant.

My first opportunity arrived in a deal meeting. Partners were discussing an acquisition structure when something caught my attention—a tax issue that echoed a scenario I'd heard about in my tax law class.

Old me would have stayed quiet and hoped someone else would notice. What if I was wrong? What if this was common knowledge and I'd look foolish for bringing it up?

New me cleared his throat and spoke up:

"Have we considered how Connecticut tax authorities might view this?"

There was a pause. I braced for humiliation. Maybe everyone already knew this. Maybe I'd misunderstood the structure entirely.

Then the partner spoke:

"Actually, that's a really good point. We should run this by the tax group before we finalize anything."

It wasn't brilliant. But it mattered. And it was mine. More importantly, people were nodding, taking notes. I'd contributed something instead of just sitting there absorbing other people's insights.

Years later, I found myself at Princeton helping run our summer intern program. Each summer brought incredibly smart students, but I recognized familiar patterns.

Take Ben. Philosophy concentration, finance certificate, thesis on ethical reasoning in markets, nearly perfect GPA. He could compare and contrast Mr. Rogers and Machiavelli off the top of his head, but ask him a direct question in a fund manager meeting? Silence.

We brought Ben and another intern on a trip through Europe. Dozens of meetings. We even did a due diligence trip to a theme park owned by one of our private equity managers. The other intern, a top MBA candidate, kicked off her heels and screamed joyfully on a rollercoaster ride during our "diligence." Ben stood quietly to the side, politely declining.

"Not a fan of heights?" I asked.

"I'm fine," he replied.

He wasn't. He was calculating safety, just like I had. The same mental math: What's the worst that could happen if I participate versus what's the worst that could happen if I don't? He was choosing the sidelines because they felt safer.

Back home, I was worried he wasn't going to get a return offer. No one had heard him speak much. I asked Ben to give a presentation to the entire investment team as a summary of the trip. Not because we needed it, but because he did.

His presentation surprised everyone. Insightful, detailed, thoughtful. The senior staff was impressed.

"Why haven't we heard these insights before?" I asked him afterward.

"I thought everyone already knew."

"Ben, we can't read your mind."

That conversation changed something. Ben started speaking, asking questions, and engaging openly. He got the return offer. He turned out to be one of our best-ever analysts, and we had almost missed out on hiring him. He worked with us for several years until his spouse's new job took him elsewhere. Today, he's thriving at one of the country's best investment firms.

He skipped the rollercoaster but finally decided to participate in everything else. Same miscalculation I'd made. Thinking the "safe choice" was actually safe.

Over the years, I watched countless interns navigate similar terrain. One clicked his pen so nervously during an interview that it sounded like a metronome. By the end of thirty minutes, everyone in the room was unconsciously nodding to the rhythm. Another showed up to our first coffee wearing an "I GOT THIS" t-shirt. Spoiler alert: He didn't. When I asked him about his interest in private equity, he launched into a story about his plans for later in the summer.

A third was so intimidated by Excel that she'd type a formula, hit enter, then physically back away from the computer—like she was waiting for it to explode. We'd sit next to her, gently walking through the basics, watching her slowly inch closer to the screen as her confidence grew.

One of my favorites was the intern who brought a legal pad to every meeting and wrote down everything. *Everything.* I once glanced over and saw her notes: "Ted said good morning. Talked about his dog." She was treating every interaction like it might be on the test later.

I began telling interns exactly what I wished I'd heard back in Hartford:

"Ask questions. Clarify expectations. Stop worrying about perfection. Aim for usefulness.

"Speak up, especially if something feels unclear. The best insights often start with the simplest questions: 'I know this might seem obvious, but...'"

The interns who succeeded weren't perfect. They were curious, engaged, and willing to risk embarrassment to actually learn something.

When students today ask me how to excel in internships, I tell them it's not entirely about the internship tasks themselves. It's also about showing up as yourself rather than a perfect version that you think others expect.

It's about the intern who asked a private equity manager, mid-pitch, "Do you think private equity is ethical?" Sure, it was awkward. But we didn't fire him. We helped him improve.

The interns who stand out aren't those trying to be perfect; they're the ones who work hard, share their thinking, and treat everyone with respect. They build relationships early, and they don't only reach out when they need something. They update the people who've helped them, even just to say thank you or share how an introduction turned out. That thoughtfulness compounds.

These lessons apply to established professionals as well. The best managers I've known aren't those with flawless answers. They're honest about their process, openly acknowledge what they don't know, and ask great questions.

They're also open to challenge—and they invite it. As you grow more senior, it's tempting to surround yourself with people who agree with you. The best leaders resist that. They create space for dissent, and they stay open to constructive criticism and new ideas.

The real skill is not flawless competence. It's authentic presence.

It took me fifteen pages of irrelevant legal analysis, silence in meetings, and a dingy conference room to understand that the real risk isn't asking a dumb question. The real risk is being so afraid of small mistakes that you guarantee a bigger one: being completely forgettable.

What Compounds

The most dangerous miscalculation I made that summer wasn't about Connecticut non-compete law. It was about risk itself. I thought staying quiet was the safe choice. *Keep your head down, don't make waves, survive the summer.* But safety and invisibility aren't the same thing. What feels like prudent caution often guarantees the very failure you're trying to avoid.

The memo disaster taught me that asking clarifying questions isn't admitting ignorance. It's showing respect for the work and the person assigning it. "What format do you need? Who's the audience? How does this fit the bigger picture?" These aren't signs of weakness. They're signs of professionalism. Over time, I came to see that what compounds in a career isn't just knowledge or technical skill—it's the willingness to show up authentically in moments of uncertainty.

The deeper lesson was about presence versus performance. The interns who succeeded, both at the law firm and later at Princeton, weren't the ones who appeared to have all the answers. They were the ones genuinely curious about the answers they didn't yet have. Every time you choose engagement over invisibility, you build a reputation for being someone worth including in important conversations. People remember who asks thoughtful questions, who admits what they don't know, and who contributes rather than just observes.

Authenticity turned out to be more valuable than perfection. The courage to say "I don't know, but here's how I'd find out" built more credibility than any amount of silent nodding ever could. This pattern repeats throughout your career. In investment meetings, the best insights often come from someone asking the obvious question everyone's thinking but afraid to voice. In client presentations, acknowledging uncertainty builds more trust than false confidence. In leadership roles, modeling curiosity creates space for others to do the same.

The interns I mentored who embraced this approach didn't just get return offers. They developed into leaders who could navigate ambiguity with confidence. They learned early that intellectual honesty is a competitive advantage, not a liability. More importantly, they avoided the trap that derails many promising careers: becoming so focused on appearing competent that you stop actually becoming more competent. Learning requires admitting what you don't know yet.

What Endures

I feel a little bad about sharing all these intern mishaps without acknowledging more of my own (and there are many). These moments seemed significant at the time, but now they just make me laugh. In college, I was an intern for Congressman Gerry Studds, the representative for my South Shore district, answering phones during the Clinton transition. When George Stephanopoulos, the famous campaign strategist, called to talk to the congressman about an early policy change, I panicked when our chief of staff told me to stall.

The first thing I thought of was how long and famously complicated his last name was, so I literally asked him to spell it. Letter by letter, painstakingly slowly. Then, I sloooowly spelled it back to him and had him confirm that I had it right.

And, I didn't just spell it, I gave a Massachusetts town name for each letter.

"S as in Stoughton? T as in Tisbury? E as in Edgartown?"..."and S as in Scituate?"

He patiently confirmed each letter for me while waiting for me to connect him to the congressman. By the time I got to the final "s," two of my colleagues were laughing so hard they were doubled over.

It was not my finest moment of political sophistication. I don't know how I held it together.

Of course, sometimes I still think about that kid in the cheap red Ford Escort, about to become a father, driving home from Hartford with his stomach in knots and wondering if he'd just blown his shot at a legal career. He got the offer. All eight summer associates did, despite the managing partner's motivational theater about limited slots. But the real education happened in those moments of failure and recovery: the memo that missed the mark, the silence that nearly cost everything, the single useful contribution that broke the spell.

Years later, watching brilliant Princeton students make the same mistakes, I realized that learning to be present instead of perfect isn't just an internship lesson. It's a life skill that determines whether you'll be someone others want to include, promote, and partner with over time.

The best part about mentoring those interns was watching them discover their own voices: Ben presenting that trip summary. The Excel-intimidated intern finally hitting enter without panicking.

They all learned what I wish I'd known at twenty-three: Your job isn't to prove you're the smartest person in the room. It's to be the most engaged. That's how you become someone people remember, trust, and want to work with again.

The old red Ford is long gone. With a baby on the way, we wanted something that felt safer. But that lesson about presence over perfection? It compounds every day.

CHAPTER 4

From Boardroom to Blackboard: Humility and the Long View

W HEN I FIRST WALKED into a Boston University classroom to teach thirty-two nineteen-year-olds the time value of money, I thought I knew what I was doing.

After all, I had spent fifteen years on the senior team managing Princeton's $34 billion endowment, co-leading its private equity and venture capital investments. I met regularly with leaders of the tech, venture capital, and private equity industries, sat on advisory boards for some of the most well-known, high-profile investment firms, and made billions of dollars for Princeton's research efforts and scholarships. My class's subject matter, the basics of finance, felt like it should be a familiar topic.

Teaching it, though, was something very different, as I was soon to learn.

My initial instinct was to lecture. I carefully presented meticulously prepared slides, explained problems from the textbook, and delivered the material the way I had approached Princeton's Board of Directors meetings: clear, logical, efficient.

After my first class, I immediately texted my family group chat that it had been a fantastic success, and I was now headed to Rowes Wharf to catch the ferry home. However, as I enjoyed a well-deserved beer on that ferry, I had a nagging feeling that my delivery had somehow failed to land.

By the second week, I saw the gap within fifteen minutes of class time. Blank stares, silence after key concepts, a classroom empty of engagement. The material wasn't the problem—it was the format. I was delivering information, not creating understanding. And crucially, I was not making room for student participation.

In the moment, I realized I needed to pivot, and now.

I took down the slide deck and put up on the screen the practice problems for today's material. I told the students to organize themselves into groups of two or three and start working on the problems together. I told them I wanted to hear noise, hear talking... I wanted to hear them helping each other. My teaching assistant and I moved around the classroom, asking what was working and what wasn't. Questions quickly began to emerge—not the superficial type, but thoughtful inquiries indicating that students were genuinely wrestling with the material.

After about twenty minutes of this chaos, I started to worry that I had lost control of the classroom. But something was shifting. The room had come alive. I gathered everyone back together and picked up a piece of chalk, pivoting to a shared group discussion. We started working through the same problems together on the chalkboard. One of the students said, "Wow—chalkboard, old school."

Then came a moment that I'll never forget. We were modeling retirement savings, comparing someone who starts saving $7,000 annually (the current max in an Individual Retirement Account in the US) at age twenty-two versus another who starts at thirty-five, and both continuing to save until age sixty-five. A student stared at his HP financial calculator and did a double take; he audibly gasped:

"Wait...the first person ends up with a million plus more?"

Heads turned. The power of compounding—one of finance's foundational concepts—suddenly felt tangible. It wasn't just a formula; it was real.

Teaching nineteen-year-olds the time value of money wasn't my original plan. With my background, I first envisioned teaching a specialized, upper-level course on endowment management or alternative investments—classes closely tied to my professional expertise. Some of my counterparts at other endowments had done this at several of the top universities in the world, and at times it felt a bit like the equivalent of an endowment manager's "flex"—teaching a highly specialized class at a prestigious school to demonstrate status. (I call it a flex partly in jest—and I'm certain these courses offer great value to advanced students.) But I had spent the last year networking with seasoned professors at BU, BC, Babson, Brandeis, HBS, and Princeton, including many who had transitioned from industry into academia, and they changed my perspective. I'm so grateful.

They made clear that understanding a subject deeply and teaching it effectively were two very distinct skill sets. Mastery of investment strategy didn't automatically translate into classroom success. In my conversations with those professors, one at BU had given me an opportunity to teach one section of Measuring Financial Value, the foundational principles of finance. At first, part of me initially felt, "Don't they know who I am? I managed billions for one of the world's leading endowments." But slowly, it dawned on me: Perhaps starting with foundational principles wasn't a consolation prize; maybe it was the best possible opportunity I could have asked for—even better than crafting my dream seminar on sophisticated endowment or family office strategies. I could use this opportunity to work on a new skill—teaching.

To be clear, teaching this class has given me an even deeper appreciation for career educators who have dedicated their professional lives to mastering the art and science of teaching. I'm very much aware that I have only begun to scratch the surface and have a tremendous amount to learn.

As I began to find my style in the classroom, I started to hear echoes of my investment philosophy. Instincts developed while managing Princeton's endowment kept surfacing: simplify to amplify, focus on quality over quantity, emphasize alignment, respect the power of time.

At Princeton, we often emphasized "fewer, better, stronger" when selecting fund managers—concentrating capital with trusted teams that delivered superior results. The same held true for teaching. Initially, I'd packed each session with multiple concepts, numerous examples, and extra problems—which I soon realized was diluting impact. Narrowing it down to two or three ideas per class and going over fewer problems more slowly, then pausing to make sure we were bringing everyone along, improved clarity dramatically.

Another lesson transcended investing and teaching alike: Timing matters, but judgment matters more. In investing, our best outcomes rarely come from perfectly timed investments. Instead, they emerge from consistently backing exceptional managers through cycles. Similarly, impactful teaching moments often arise unexpectedly—a hesitant student's question or a spontaneous small-group discussion that I opened to the entire class when we regrouped, reshaping everyone's understanding.

Good outcomes require more than good structure. They demand genuine engagement.

Later in the semester, while discussing perpetuities, I decided to use a university endowment as an example. Endowments are essentially perpetuities, structured to last indefinitely. They are designed to both meaningfully support today's students and research efforts and to preserve the endowment's purchasing power forever. Students were amazed to discover that institutions like Princeton—with its $34 billion endowment—couldn't simply spend more to immediately fill budget gaps or eliminate tuition entirely without negatively affecting future generations. As an aside, this tension has intensified recently, as university endowments grapple with unprecedented challenges and threats. Navigating these pressures while maintaining intergenerational equity requires precisely the long-term discipline and clarity I was trying to teach.

The more I tied the concepts to real-world examples, the greater the students' comprehension. Suddenly, the time value of money wasn't merely a test topic—it became the fundamental rationale of retirement plans, student loans, and mortgages that they will encounter throughout life.

The abstract became concrete, even personal.

During one of my office hours, I asked a student for feedback on how the class was going, and she remarked, "I always thought finance was just formulas and Excel. But you talk a lot about people and retirement savings and career advice."

That was the moment I understood teaching finance wasn't just about delivering skills—how to use the time value of money keys on their Hewlett-Packard financial calculators. It was about instilling a long-term mindset, empowering students to make wise decisions even amid uncertainty.

Today, teaching is one of several professional activities I navigate. I invest a private fund alongside a longtime Princeton colleague. I advise family offices and venture capital firms across the US and Europe. And I teach.

Rather than stepping away from investment management into academia (which many have successfully and rewardingly done), I've come to see teaching, investing, and advising as mutually reinforcing. Each strengthens the others. What surprised me was how much they fed each other. I call it my "portfolio life."

Teaching demands clarity. You can't hide behind a great track record, name-dropping, or complexity with nineteen-year-olds—

you must truly grasp an idea to explain it simply. That's a valuable discipline, particularly in investing.

Investing, meanwhile, grounds my teaching. Real-world experiences enrich classroom discussions, showing students how finance concepts play out when the stakes are in the billions. My advisory work with family offices and nonprofits similarly reinforces decision-making clarity across varied contexts. These conversations underscore how even the most robust financial models must accommodate human needs, desires, and values.

At Princeton, our mandate was intergenerational equity—allocating capital prudently today without compromising the future. Teaching mirrors this responsibility closely.

Every classroom interaction—every story I tell, every moment of a student's insight—is an investment. Returns are rarely immediate. But then a student asks another question, makes a connection, or realizes they're not just absorbing financial concepts—they're learning to think long-term.

I never intentionally brought my endowment investment philosophy into first-year finance classes. But perhaps I've spent so much time and effort in the endowment world that I bring it into all I do. Managing capital and teaching rely on remarkably similar fundamentals: patience, purpose—and above all, the discipline to think long-term.

What Compounds

Teaching quickly humbled me. Subject matter expertise and teaching skills are not the same thing—and the humility required to bridge that gap is significant. I had spent fifteen years in rooms where my credibility was assumed: Elite investment firms sought my opinion, I shaped billions in portfolio decisions, and my institutional title carried weight. Then I walked into a room full of nineteen-year-olds and realized none of that mattered. I had to earn their trust, their engagement, and their effort from scratch. That was humbling—and liberating.

The best teachers don't just know the content—they know how to listen. Listening to what's not being said in a classroom—the silence after a confusing concept, the hesitation in a student's question, the unspoken overwhelm—became as important as delivering content. It reminded me of due diligence meetings, where what a manager didn't say was often as telling as what they did.

That kind of listening builds empathy, and empathy compounds. Sitting in front of a room of students with different levels of preparation, different backgrounds, and different aspirations deepened how I approach leadership, team building, and mentorship. Good teachers—and good managers—don't expect everyone to be at the same point. They meet people where they are and help them move forward.

Moving among teaching, investing, and advising has given me a wider lens—and that diversity of activities has made me better at each of them. Teaching sharpens my clarity of thought, investing deepens my judgment, and advising broadens my perspective. The interplay keeps me curious and adaptable and helps prevent the tunnel vision that can come from doing just one thing. Like a well-built investment portfolio, the mix of roles has made the whole stronger than the sum of its parts.

I also learned that finance isn't truly understood until it feels personal. I had spent years modeling institutional cash flows, optimizing fund allocations, and managing long-duration capital. But when a student gasps aloud at the power of compounding for their own retirement, it's a different kind of return on investment. It's not just a return on capital—it's a return on understanding.

Clarity compounds. The act of explaining something to someone encountering it for the first time sharpened me, not only as a teacher but also as an investor, board member, and advisor. If you can explain it to a nineteen-year-old, you can explain it to anyone.

Structure is important, but responsiveness is essential. My first instinct was to tightly control each class session, mirroring the precision I brought to investment committees. But real learning often happens in the moments when you loosen your grip—when you make space for conversation, improvisation, and curiosity. That flexibility, both in teaching and investing, builds confidence. Not the head-of-the-boardroom confidence, but the confidence that comes from watching students grow, from seeing abstract concepts land, and from letting go of perfection in favor of presence.

Discipline matters too. Just like in investing, good teaching is about showing up consistently, preparing rigorously, reflecting honestly, and being patient about results. You don't get immediate feedback from a compounding portfolio—or from a first-year class. But over time, the returns reveal themselves. In a thank-you email. In a surprising office hours conversation. In a student who chooses a career path they never considered before.

Perhaps most of all, I learned that teaching is not about transmitting knowledge—it's about expanding perspective. My students may forget the formula for a perpetuity. But if they remember how it felt to realize they could build wealth, take control of their financial future, or teach someone else—that will stay with them far longer than any midterm grade. And that's what gives teaching its own kind of purpose. Investing for an endowment gave me purpose by supporting research, scholarships, and the long-term mission of a university. Teaching has given me a new one: helping young people develop a mindset that can shape their lives. The two aren't mutually exclusive. In fact, they reinforce each other. Purpose layered on purpose is how meaning deepens.

What Endures

Life can take you to fascinating and unexpected places when you stay open, stay curious, and start small. I remember a Princeton undergrad named Peter, a Mechanical and Aerospace Engineering (MAE) concentrator who showed up to a Princo career fair info session on a whim. He had planned to apply to somewhere like Boeing or Raytheon, but was curious about what the endowment team did. We spoke at the session, and he asked some of the most thoughtful questions I've heard from an undergrad.

His résumé didn't make it through the initial screen (an analyst wrote in his notes: Why would an MAE major want to do finance?), but I used to review the first screen rejects at home over the weekend, just to be sure we didn't miss someone unconventional. I spotted Peter's résumé, noting he'd mentioned our conversation in his cover letter. We put him in the interview pool. Peter crushed it and became one of the best analysts in Princo history.

That experience launched him into the investing world, first with us, focusing on our public markets managers, and eventually joining a successful hedge fund. Had he skipped that session, or had I not read his entire cover letter, his path might've gone another way. Small choices at the time, big outcomes.

So much of success, especially early in your career, isn't about picking the perfect destination. It's about building the habits, relationships, and perspective that give you more options over time. That's what compounds: trust, effort, clarity, resilience, curiosity.

Thinking long-term is a competitive advantage. It's true in investing, and it's true in life. There's an old saying—so common it's almost cliché—that people overestimate what they can do in a week and underestimate what they can do in a decade. You have time—use it wisely.

And don't underestimate the quiet decisions. The class you agree to teach. The meeting where you stay after to ask a better question. The person you mentor even when you feel unqualified. These moments are small, but they multiply.

At the end of the day, your impact won't come just from what you know. It will come from what you choose to share, how you choose to lead, and whether you help others understand things they didn't before.

In the boardroom, returns are measured in dollars. In the classroom, they're measured in moments of understanding.

Both require humility. Both require the long view.

PART II

Compounding Capital

I'M A PATIENT PERSON in many parts of life. I built a career managing long-term capital, investing with decades-long horizons, and thinking carefully about risk and return across generations.

But put me in a restaurant with a wait time, and that patience evaporates instantly. I won't wait for a table under any circumstances. If there's a crowd by the host stand, I'm already walking out the door. My family has come to accept this as one of my many, many quirks. I'll happily spend the entire evening hopping from place to place in search of a zero-minute wait, convinced, perhaps irrationally, that the restaurant should feel lucky to seat us, not the other way around.

It's not my finest trait. But it does underscore something funny: In the part of my life (besides parenting!) that has required the most discipline and long-term thinking, I've had to actively train myself to embrace patience. It wasn't automatic. It was learned.

That's what Part II is really about. Not specific investment strategies or financial formulas, but the principles that make compounding capital possible—the judgment to choose wisely, the conviction to stand by your decisions, and the patience to let them grow.

Capital isn't just about money, though we measure it in numbers. It's about possibility and potential. It's about funding ideas, innovations, and institutions to thrive beyond their current boundaries. During my years managing Princeton's private equity and venture capital portfolios, I came to deeply appreciate the intricate interplay of risk and return, patience and action, analysis and intuition. I learned that great investing isn't about predicting the future, but rather about preparing for it—about positioning yourself thoughtfully so you're ready when opportunities inevitably arise.

The principles governing successful long-term investing mirror the principles that govern successful living. The patience required to let investments mature teaches us about delayed gratification in career building. The discipline of thorough due diligence translates to careful decision-making in relationships. The courage to make contrarian bets when you believe in something reflects the same courage needed to pursue unconventional paths in life.

The choices we make about where and how to invest reveal what we value most deeply. Behind every number on a spreadsheet is a decision about who or what merits our trust, attention, and resources. These decisions shape not only portfolios but entire communities, fields of research, and generations of students and leaders.

This is especially true with endowments. Thoughtfully managed, endowments can power extraordinary progress, funding groundbreaking research, supporting talented scholars, expanding educational access, and fueling innovations that change the world. The impact of compounding capital through an endowment can ripple outward for generations, creating legacies far beyond immediate financial returns.

In this section, we'll explore stories from the investment world not as financial advice, but as windows into timeless principles about patience, judgment, and the power of thinking beyond immediate results. We'll see how financial strategy, when thoughtfully executed, can set change in motion, creating legacies that far outlive short-term cycles. Because ultimately, I've come to see compounding capital as less about accumulating wealth than it is about expanding possibility and enabling human potential to flourish, sustainably, across time.

And maybe it's a reminder that the best returns, like the best tables, are often worth the wait.

CHAPTER 5

The One for Sale: Reframing Risk, Earning Trust

M Y FIRST PRINCO OFFICE had all the charm of a storage closet that someone gave up on halfway through converting. It had a view of a parking garage, green duct tape holding the carpet together, an unexplained hole in the wall, and a faint whiff of mildew that might've come from the ceiling tiles. There was, in fact, what looked like mold on the ceiling, but no one was willing to get close enough to confirm. If this was Princeton's idea of a welcome mat, I was already wondering what I had walked into.

At Lincoln, I'd had an office on the forty-first floor of a new glass tower in Philadelphia with a panoramic view of the Art Museum. One of my first days there, I'd looked out over the Rocky steps and thought: *This is pretty good.* Now, two weeks into the job at Princeton, I was wondering if I'd gone backwards. I'd made a big move, and here

I was, with a lesser title, a moldy ceiling, a parking deck view, and a pit in my stomach.

But during that summer of 2008, aesthetic discomfort was the least of anyone's concerns. Banks were starting to buckle. Markets were sliding. And at Princeton, we were staring at a quieter but equally dangerous problem: We were overcommitted to private equity and venture capital funds. By a lot.

Before I joined, the prior three years had been a golden era for PE and VC fundraising. Bigger funds, bigger commitments, a lot of excitement. Now the bill was coming due, and those commitments were a liability sitting on the balance sheet. Typically, a slow-moving problem, but one that could hit all at once.

I was brand new at the endowment, still learning everyone's names, when I asked what I thought was a simple, relevant question.

"Have we thought about secondaries?"

The room froze.

Secondaries are the buying and selling of fund interests before they naturally mature. Because they are quite illiquid, they often sell at a discount to net asset value. After a long silence, the CIO, Andy, and the MD at the time debated over who would get to answer.

For fifteen minutes, they explained—firmly, publicly—why we would not consider secondaries. It ran counter to everything Princeton stood for. We were the ultimate long-term partner. We didn't trade relationships. Andy had a phrase for our strategy: the BLT, Beyond the Long-Term. Selling LP interests was what panicked institutions did. It was reactionary. It was shortsighted. It was not Princeton. Indeed, Princeton had a goal of being every GP's favorite LP.

I walked out of that meeting thinking I'd made a massive mistake. I'd come in with what I thought was a useful perspective. I left feeling like an idiot. One of those moments where you question if you're even cut out for the job.

One week later, they walked into my dingy office and asked me to tell them everything I knew about secondaries.

When I saw them heading toward my office, my first thought wasn't curiosity. It was dread. What did I screw up? They didn't acknowledge the lecture from the previous week. They just launched into it.

"How visible is the seller in the process?"

"What does it look like to structure a quiet deal?"

"How public does this get?"

What they were really asking was: Can this be done without anyone knowing? We had a problem. And, while they weren't ready to say so out loud, they were starting to think secondaries might be the solution. Now they were coming to the new guy in the worst office on campus to help them figure it out.

That summer, my wife and I had been trying to find a house in Princeton. At the time, Princeton real estate was a tough market, as almost nothing was coming up for sale. We toured one place that felt wildly overpriced, especially as the financial world was unraveling. We passed. Ten months later, the same house was still on the market—only now it was 25 percent cheaper. We bought it, mainly because it was the only house for sale in the same elementary district as the house we'd been renting, and we didn't want the kids to have to switch schools again.

It needed work. It had a 1980s aesthetic—a little worn down, a little confusing. But it had history: Nobel prize-winning novelist Toni Morrison had once lived there, and the kitchen still had these colorful, slightly eccentric tiles she may have commissioned. The bones were good. It just needed a lot of updating.

We hired a Romanian contractor, Eugen, who was cheerful, hard-working, and played Romanian music all day while his subcontractors made creative decisions. One of the plumbers had gotten his license the same day he started on our job. His quote was very reasonable, almost cheap. A more established Princeton plumber, who had an office on Nassau Street (the high-rent district), gave a quote for the same job at three times the amount. We went with the newly licensed guy. His wife went into labor at 9 p.m. one night while he was working late on our bathroom, which was in pieces. That same night, two hours later, his apprentice (who had been working alone upstairs) appeared in the living room looking as if he had just jumped into a pool. He said everything was fine.

At some point during that renovation, my young son asked why we bought this house. "Because it was the only one for sale," Liz and I said in unison.

That logic was oddly similar to the secondaries work I was doing at Princeton. Not everything about it felt perfect. It went against some of our best instincts. But it was what was available, and we had to make the best of it.

Amid the renovation dust and the tension at work, we needed something that reminded us why we were here as a family. That summer in Princeton wasn't just about work and renovations. We quickly discovered that the campus was perfect for bike riding with the kids. Nearly every weekend, especially that first year, we set off to explore every corner of campus—racing across the open stretch of Poe Field, coasting down the gradual decline of Shapiro Walk, and taking a break next to the fountain of Prospect Gardens. Those rides became one of our favorite weekend rituals, and long after the stress of that move faded, they're what I remember most.

They were our pause button—a way to remember what mattered while everything else felt like it was coming apart. And, while our house was in pieces, our PE commitments felt like they might buckle under the pressure.

Back to the secondaries.

I like working in stages. Think first, then move. Having a standing weekly PE meeting gave me structure. A rhythm for incremental progress. The first step was defining the problem. Decisions needed to be made about what to sell. I started by ruling out selling venture capital. That was easy. No way we'd get fair value in that market. Plus, it is very hard to know if a portfolio includes a winning lottery ticket.

Next: top-tier buyout managers—the large firms that bought whole companies, with both equity and debt, and promised to fix them. These firms were central to Princeton's strategy. Selling them would send the wrong signal.

At the bottom were the messy ones. Troubled managers, poor performance, personnel issues. Those would require deep discounts. Save them for later.

That left the middle. The decent-but-not-exceptional buyout managers. Not core, not catastrophic. Just right for secondaries, if one needed to do them. That was our opportunity set.

Then I stepped back and asked: *What problem are we really solving?* We didn't need cash now. The university's operational budget wasn't the issue. The real risk was that capital calls (the money we promised to send to firms) would keep coming, but distributions (the money they'd send back to us) would stop. That's what happens in a downturn. The net-cash-flow treadmill doesn't slow down. It speeds up.

So I reframed the goal. It wasn't to raise cash. It was to de-risk the balance sheet. Then I asked myself: *How much would we pay to undo these commitments?* That gave me a mental exchange rate. If someone was willing to take the uncalled commitment off our hands, I could accept a meaningful discount on each fund's net asset value, or NAV. Because I wasn't just selling assets. I was unloading liabilities, and the price for shedding these liabilities was the dollar value of the discount.

Same transaction. Different lens.

I brought that framework to the next PE meeting. I walked the team through it. The buckets. The rationale. The idea of measuring success not by price to NAV, but by how many dollars we "spent" to de-risk each commitment.

Andy, the CIO, leaned back. "How much would I pay to undo these commitments?" He paused. "A lot."

He was in.

At one of the next meetings, someone suggested using a broker. "Might help shield our name." That triggered every alarm in me. A broker with Princeton as a client? That's not discretion—that's marketing gold for them. They'd use us on every pitch deck they made for the next year. "Trusted by the best," etc.

So I came up with another plan. Instead of a broker, I called three or four secondary buyers I knew personally. People with discretion. People who didn't need to be told how serious confidentiality was. I told them, "If this leaks, you're out."

But I didn't just threaten them—I sold them. I told them, "If you handle this discreetly, you get something rare: the chance to tell your own LPs confidentially that you saw proprietary deal flow directly from a top-tier endowment. No intermediary. No publicity. Just access." It worked.

We also did something unusual. Most LPs wait to tell GPs about something like a secondary sale. We told them early. "The world's changed. We overcommitted. We might need to sell. But it's not because we don't believe in you."

We asked who they'd want to see on their LP roster. Who was their ideal buyer? Not only did they appreciate the transparency, but they also gave us names. Firms that had been hounding them for more allocation, asking about secondaries, looking for coinvests. We made sure one of those names was in the bidding group, quietly and strategically.

It was the right thing to do. And it helped the deal.

We also approached a few GPs about resizing their funds. "You could take 20–25 percent off everyone's commitment," we said. "The world's changed. You probably need less." Because of our relationships and the credibility of the ask, many said yes.

All told: a staggering amount of liquidity, quietly created. No leaks. No signals. No drama. Just quiet execution. And it changed how people saw me.

What Compounds

Asking the right question at the wrong time can feel like a mistake until it turns out to be the question everyone needs to ask. Institutions don't always change through debate; sometimes they shift through execution. You show, you don't tell.

The way you frame something matters, too. If I'd led with, "Here's the discount we'll take," I would've lost the room. But "What would we pay to fix this?" changed the conversation. Same facts. Better story.

During that time, life at Princo was even more complex than the story in this chapter. Six weeks after I started at Princo, the head of PE announced he was leaving. News leaked quickly, and a recruiter from Boston—where I'd nearly taken another job when considering Princo—called to see if I wanted to reconsider. It was tempting: closer to my extended family and potentially more lucrative. In those first few months, I wasn't even sure I belonged at Princo or that my family and I belonged in Princeton. I called Rich, one of my bosses from Lincoln. I've often found that when you're unsettled, reaching out to a mentor can clarify what matters. Rich told me to stay where I'd learn the most, not jump to a shop that might not survive the storm in the markets. His words steadied me.

Still, I worried. If the departing MD had brought me in, what did his leaving mean for me? That's when Jon—the most respected voice on the Princo team—came by my office. "I'm sure his leaving was a surprise," he said. "But Andy and I want you here—as part of our endowment team, not just his PE team. And with him moving on, it gives you the chance to have even more impact." Jon wasn't someone who talked just to fill the silence. When he speaks, people listen. His words didn't just steady me—they gave me a sense that I could grow into more than I'd expected.

Not long after, Jon's wife invited Liz and Andy's wife to breakfast. Jon's wife had a warmth and kindness that made people feel at ease, and that day, they offered Liz their own reassurance. It made both of us feel a little less like outsiders. Reflecting on it now, the spouses were often called on to support Princo in their own ways too—quietly, and often without recognition. That breakfast was one of those moments.

Looking back, those gestures—Rich's advice, Jon's reassurance, Jon's wife's kind invitation—might seem small. But they landed with an outsized impact. In periods of uncertainty, they signaled belonging, and they built confidence. And just like compounding, it's those small, repeated acts of trust and encouragement that add up.

At places obsessed with big thinking, what really compounds is follow-through—the late-night spreadsheets, the quiet calls, the meetings you don't brag about. You do the unglamorous work, and then you disappear into the background again, ready to pitch in on the next challenge. Over time, that's how trust builds. I started as the new guy, asking dumb questions. I ended up owning and solving the problem. Not because I had the boldest vision, but because I stuck with it and delivered.

Just as important, discretion mattered. And relationships deepened in the process. The calls we made to GPs, the way we told the story—it turned a desperate move into a credible one. Over time, people don't just remember what you fixed. They remember how you handled it.

The more you show you can solve a problem without leaks or theatrics, the more people hand you the problems that actually matter.

Judgment compounds, too. It wasn't just what we did, but how we did it—who we told, how we framed it, the restraint we showed, the care we took. That kind of discernment builds slowly. Then suddenly, people see you differently.

And in that process, your identity starts to change. This was the moment I stopped being the new ex-lawyer turned investor guy and started being someone who could steer through ambiguity. It showed up in the tone of meetings, in what people assumed I could handle, and in the responsibilities I was invited into next.

What Endures

Over the years, the stigma around selling LP interests has faded dramatically. The secondary market itself has matured—scaled buyers, greater liquidity, and more transparent processes mean that selling is no longer viewed as a mark of distress but often as a strategic portfolio management tool. More than fifteen years on, most institutions don't hesitate to use secondaries when reallocating capital. What once felt like an act of desperation is now seen as an accepted, even prudent, way to adapt.

In our case, there was no victory lap. No one updated their LinkedIn to say, "Led major secondary program." No happy hour to celebrate the closings. A few people noticed, but most just moved on, which was fine with me. But something shifted. Quietly, people took note.

It reminded me of that house Liz and I bought—the one we never planned on, the one that felt wrong at the moment, until it turned out to be the only move that made sense. It wasn't perfect, but it was what was available. And over time, with work, it became something we could build on.

The same was true with our secondary sale. It was a mess. And we managed to clean it up. Not because it was easy, but because it had to be done.

Sometimes what compounds isn't capital, but credibility.

And sometimes, it all starts with asking a question at the exact wrong moment, and sticking around long enough to make it right. Like the house we never planned to buy, it wasn't perfect. But it was the one for sale. And in making it work, we adapted—and came out stronger for it.

CHAPTER 6

Fewer, Better, Stronger:
Building Real Partnerships

I T WAS FEBRUARY 2009. A snowstorm had rolled into Boston just after I had flown in from Princeton to meet with a manager. The global financial crisis was still in full swing, and while the official reason for the trip was work, the night after the meeting was for family. And for hockey.

I had tickets to a Bruins game with three of my cousins—Matt, Joe, and John. It was the kind of night that made all the chaos of the job momentarily fade: burgers, beers, jokes flying in every direction. We all grew up with modest backgrounds, public schools, hardworking parents. We had strong values, stronger loyalty, and a sense that we were in it together. Nobody in our circle went to Princeton or Harvard or Yale. Those places were like another planet.

Somewhere between my second beer and a round of teasing about something dumb I'd done as a kid, we found ourselves talking about our Aunt Re's desserts—seven-layer bars, peanut butter M&M balls, and rainbow marshmallow chocolate slices (aka marshmallow things). Just naming them made me smile; it transported me.

As a kid, I spent quite a few weekends at their family's cabin up in New Hampshire, "babysitting" my cousins. In reality, I was only a few years older than them, and I suspect that Aunt Re and Uncle Roger really brought me along to help me escape a challenging home life and quietly fold me into something steady and kind.

That house, those weekends. They were awesome. Those memories have stuck with me through every phase of life. Looking back, those weekends may have been my first real lesson in what trust felt like. Not earned. Just offered.

At some point during the night at the Bruins game, the tone shifted. One of them asked about our move for the new job. "So, seriously... Princeton, huh? What's that like?"

I told them the truth. "It feels like another planet. Some days I feel like an alien."

But under the laughter, I felt a tension I hadn't named yet—because while I belonged here with them, I wasn't sure I belonged in Princeton. In Boston, even when people are blunt, they're direct in a way that signals respect. You know where you stand. There's a camaraderie, like we're all on the same team, even if we're giving each other crap. Princeton was... different.

Princeton, the university, was extraordinary—brilliant students, world-class research, and colleagues who pushed me to grow every day. Princeton, the town, however, was something else entirely. It was polite, or perhaps proper, but in a way that was meant to exclude. If someone asked how I was doing and I said, "Good, thanks, how about you?" they'd almost always respond, "I'm WELL, thank you."

Little corrections like that happened constantly. Tiny reminders that I didn't quite belong. Some days in Princeton, it felt like everyone was looking out for themselves. Other days, like there was a private club I didn't know the rules to. I could function there, even succeed, but belong? That was more complicated.

The next morning came fast. One night, I was surrounded by cousins and laughter; the next, back into the storm of work.

I was up early with my colleague Jim, heading to Logan Airport. He joined Princo just a few months after I did, and over the next fifteen years, he became one of my truest partners—and one of the best things to ever happen to me professionally. He'd grown up on the Jersey Shore, rowed for Yale, and never lost his fierce Bulldog pride—he even kept a bulldog statue in his backyard pointed toward the Princeton crews on Lake Carnegie. But despite his Yale loyalties, he threw himself fully into helping Princeton succeed, eventually amassing what might be the largest collection of orange ties anyone has ever assembled.

Jim was tall, loud-voiced, and full of stories. More than that, he was the kind of colleague who made you better—generous with credit, unstoppable at building relationships (a superpower in the VC world), and unfailingly optimistic. He made work fun. Even in the most stressful stretches, he could lift the room, open doors through his network, and somehow make it all feel doable. Working alongside him shaped me as an investor, a teammate, and a leader. He made even the toughest trips easier, and the biggest challenges feel shared.

On the ride to the airport, snow was still coming down hard. When we got there, all flights were canceled. I floated the idea of staying another night, having a bit more time with family. Jim shook his head and said, "We're heading to South Station." We caught the Amtrak south.

That ride turned out to be one of the most peaceful I've ever had on the train. The snow muffled everything. The world felt slowed down for once. We had space to think, and for the first time in a long while, we weren't triaging.

As we settled into the train, I pulled out a Ziplock full of Liz's homemade gingerbread cookies to share. They'd become a bit of a fixture in our office. Jim, Peter, and John swore they made meetings better. Something about them helped everyone relax, and I figured they might do the same here. They did. We started talking. About the travel. About the exhaustion. We pulled out our calendars and started going over our overloaded travel schedule for the upcoming spring annual meeting season. Each of our managers (the outside investment firms that managed the private equity and venture funds that we invested in) had an annual meeting, and one of us would need to attend each of them. Five trips each to the West Coast. Jim had China and India coming up; I was handling London. Plus, the usual: multiple trips to Boston and NYC. All in the span of a few months.

"This is brutal," I said, staring at the calendar.

"Well, we'll both have Global Services elite status on United Airlines before you know it," Jim replied.

We laughed, but it wasn't funny. All that travel meant no time in the office to develop our junior team, something we took deep pride in. We loved training recent grads into investors. But how could we mentor them if we were never there?

The conversation turned. What if we could have just as much PE and VC in the portfolio, but with fewer managers? What if we didn't have to deal with the managers who weren't true partners?

We weren't just talking about logistics anymore. We were talking about philosophy. And we didn't know it yet, but that train was carrying us toward one.

―――――――――

Back at the office, I can still picture the conference room where the idea crystallized. Dingy carpet held together with duct tape (yes, more creative use of duct tape in the office). A wooden table with splinters sharp enough to catch your tie. Chairs with stuffing poking through. The Princo office's shabbiness was no accident. Andy, our CIO, was entrusted with tens of billions in capital, but didn't want to look like it. He drove an old car and often dressed like an Ivy League professor—rumpled, unbothered, and above material signals. The offices followed the same script: threadbare carpets and furniture that looked like it had been rescued from the curb. It was theater, but theater with a purpose. Andy believed an endowment should project stewardship and restraint, not the trappings of a hedge fund. The message was clear: Every dollar was going to the mission. That frugality set a tone, but underneath the threadbare carpets, real tension was building in the portfolio itself.

(As Andy's own confidence deepened, the modesty that once defined him faded and was replaced by a growing embrace of the status and recognition that came with the role. Years later, the office followed suit, no longer sending a message of austerity, but of permanence and pride.)

In 2009, we had bigger problems than office furniture. At that point, we weren't fine-tuning models. We were triaging.

Distribution notices were down. Valuations were dropping fast. Annual meetings were stacking up. We were staring at a bloated roster of private equity and venture capital managers, and diversification wasn't protecting us. It was making our jobs harder.

That Monday, we talked about the train conversation at our PE team meeting. Everyone was nodding in agreement. This wasn't about being picky. It was about paring back the bloated list of managers we'd inherited.

In our senior team huddle afterward, we returned to something that had come up on the train: If we're always on the road, how do we invest in our own people? If we're spread too thin, how do we build anything lasting?

And so we started asking the real questions. Whom do we actually trust? Which managers are transparent, steady, and pragmatic? Who tells the truth, even when it's ugly? Who treats us like partners, not just capital providers?

Having more managers wasn't making us safer. It was spreading us too thin. Too much noise. Too many check-ins, not enough real conversations.

We started saying it out loud, informally at first: We need fewer managers. Better ones. Stronger relationships. At this point, it wasn't a theme or mantra yet, but we knew what we needed to do.

———

Then one day, back in that same conference room, Andy—who had a gift for clarity at just the right moments—said it. He looked around the room and said quietly, "Fewer. Better. Stronger." The room went still. That was it.

We weren't looking for more names on a roster. We were looking for real partnerships with people whose judgment we trusted, whose values aligned with ours, who could navigate complexity and still sleep at night.

Fewer relationships meant we could go deeper. We could mentor our team. We could spend time with our best managers when things weren't urgent, which, it turns out, is when trust is built.

Yes, we ended up more concentrated. But we didn't manage risk by adding managers. We managed it by backing ones who built their own portfolios with conviction.

Fewer. Better. Stronger. It became a filter. A compass. A culture.

In the years that followed, the strategy proved itself. We had fewer managers, but stronger partnerships. Our travel dropped by a third— less time on planes, more time in the office with our junior team. The work felt more focused, more sustainable. And the portfolio got stronger too: With our attention on highest-conviction managers, performance rebounded more quickly and steadily through the recovery.

Looking back, I don't know how I could have done this job without Liz at home with the kids. The travel and board prep were relentless; the job was all-consuming. It worked only because she held everything together. When people compliment our kids, I always credit her. Her steady devotion to our family was an act of love and partnership, and I'm convinced it's why our kids have grown into the grounded, kind people they are. In many ways, Liz modeled the very thing we were striving for in our work: a partnership built on trust, steadiness, and shared purpose. I've also come to appreciate that not everyone has that kind of support, which makes the people who carry those loads without it all the more remarkable.

What Compounds

Crisis forces clarity. When everything is falling apart, you discover what actually matters. And what matters isn't how many relationships you have, but how deep those relationships are. Diversification can be a false comfort when it spreads you too thin to build real partnerships. Better to have fewer, stronger relationships than many weak ones.

The best GPs don't want transactional LPs. They want partners—people who understand what they're trying to build and can be helpful beyond just providing capital. Every mediocre relationship crowds out space for an excellent one. Every relationship you maintain out of obligation takes energy away from one that could be transformative. Learning to say no is as important as learning when to say yes.

Over time, conviction compounds. With fewer, better relationships, you can go deeper. You can have real conversations. You can build trust that survives disagreement and partnership that survives stress. Quality compounds faster than quantity. The managers we kept were better performers and better partners. They shared opportunities they wouldn't have shared with transactional LPs. They gave us insights into markets and trends that helped across our entire portfolio.

Focus sharpens into expertise. Concentrating on fewer relationships sharpens our judgment. We became better at pattern recognition, better at asking the right questions, better at spotting problems before they became crises. And intentionality expanded, too. The more deliberate we became about where to invest our time and attention, the better we got at recognizing what deserved both.

What Endures

Sometimes I think about that Bruins night. About sitting at the bar, surrounded by laughter and long memories, talking about Aunt Re's desserts and memories at the cabin, and feeling, for once, completely at ease.

That kind of connection—unpolished, loyal, a little messy—is what real trust feels like. It's also what most investor–manager relationships *don't* feel like, but what they should.

And I think about that train ride the next morning. Everything snowed in, everything slowed down. That was the moment the signal came through the noise. That's when we started realizing that the portfolio we needed wasn't about coverage. It was about conviction.

We'd been so busy managing relationships, we'd forgotten how to build them.

Whether you're investing capital, time, or care, the principle holds. Fewer. Better. Stronger. Sometimes the best things in life—like trust, like real partnership, like Aunt Re's marshmallow things—can't be rushed or forced. They just have to be genuine.

CHAPTER 7

Building Conviction: Permission, Forgiveness, and Billion-Dollar Bets

THE VENTURE CAPITAL FIRM COO pinged me on a Tuesday afternoon. I was buried in cold inbound pitches, most of which were destined for polite declines (often in the form of "It's not you, it's me"). His email was brief and efficient—the kind you send when you're already moving and just need the other person to keep up:

"The firm co-founders will be in NYC next week. Any chance we could swing by Princeton if there's interest?"

I paused. Interesting that he had reached out to me rather than my MD or CIO. I was still a relatively new senior associate in the endowment office. This was 2009. But clearly, our recent visit to their Bay Area office left an impression. I suppose that they thought I was their most receptive audience at Princeton.

It also meant I had about ten minutes to decide whether I was going to ignore protocol.

The safe move? Forward the email to Andy, our CIO, and ask if we want to engage. Put it on the agenda for our next PE team meeting. Let the process do what the process does.

But I knew how that conversation would go. Jim, the MD, would mention how one of the VC firm founders had practically hung up on him during Fund I negotiations. Someone would cite the high fees. Andy would start stroking his beard, his version of the storm warning.

By the time we finished debating, the founders would be back in the Bay Area, and Fund II would be in motion, without us again.

I started typing before I could overthink it.

"Yes, absolutely. What time works best? We'll make it happen."

Send.

My heart rate spiked as the screen refreshed. Now I had to figure out how I was going to explain this to Andy. At an institution where relationships and process mattered almost as much as performance, this wasn't just a scheduling mishap—it was exactly the kind of protocol breach that could mark you as someone whom the CIO couldn't trust with bigger decisions. And that was not a good place to be, as I had already seen others learn the hard way.

We had first met the co-founders of this VC firm a year earlier for lunch at the SFO DoubleTree before the launch of Fund I. A trusted partner at one of the VC industry's oldest and most successful firms had made the introduction. "They're doing something different," he said.

Beige walls, industrial carpet, overhead jet noise. A hotel restaurant designed by a committee that must've hated joy. And yet, the two founders made that bland room feel like the center of the venture universe.

They weren't just pitching a fund. They were building a firm they wished had existed when they were company founders—one that actually did the things other firms claimed to do but rarely executed on. They'd use management fees to hire real support staff: talent, marketing, operations. They'd invest as a team, not a loose confederation of individuals. They had big ideas, strong convictions, and great chemistry.

They spoke like operators who had scars. They wanted to rewire venture itself. Not just write checks, but build infrastructure around founders. They planned to take no current compensation so they could fund the services. They complemented each other well: one deeply technical, and the other a skilled operator and chief executive.

"Every VC says they add value beyond capital," one said. "We're going to staff it."

What struck me most wasn't their pedigree. It was how intently they listened. They were pitching, but they were also learning, curious about our people-first approach to GP-LP partnerships. That wasn't typical VC behavior.

Most VCs pitch track records. These guys pitched values—a truly founder-first VC firm.

Jim was intrigued, but cautious. His VC instincts kicked in. He had been a VC for twenty-five years before joining the endowment world, and was currently navigating the tricky GP to LP transition. He noted that terms were rich, they were unproven, and one of the co-founders had already rubbed him the wrong way.

We stayed in touch. Then came Fund I discussions.

It unraveled fast.

The terms weren't just above market. They were aspirational. High fees, high carry. It was almost like they were told that if they wanted to be a top-tier firm, they had to have top-tier terms. They had a point.

"But they're not a top-tier firm yet," Jim said. "They're two guys with a deck and a heck of a lot of confidence."

The final call sealed it. I wasn't on the line, but word spread fast: The technical VC grew frustrated, said something like "Maybe we're not the right fit," and abruptly ended the call with Jim.

End of Fund I, and our chance to participate.

A few weeks later, Jim walked by my office holding a magazine cover; he spoke no words at first, just held it like a wanted poster. The technical VC founder was splashed across a business magazine, striking a pose that made him look larger than life. Then, Jim said, "Bye-bye, Princeton!"

I frankly had no idea what he meant, but I laughed anyway—mostly because Jim was laughing, and his laughter was infectious. So I just joined in.

But I couldn't stop wondering: What if we'd been wrong? What if we got too caught up in the terms negotiations, had our feelings hurt, and were missing out on something amazing? That curiosity lingered. If they really were building something new, I wanted to see for myself.

When we planned the next West Coast trip, I added them to the itinerary. Just to keep the relationship warm.

"Why?" Jim asked.

"Because they're going to raise Fund II," I said. "And we should want the option for a second shot."

Their office was modern, full of energy. But what struck me was the bold art near the entrance—something that made clear they meant to disrupt. Subtlety was not their strong suit.

We didn't get a pitch that day. Just a conversation with the operator VC and their new COO. They showed us how the platform was taking shape. Actual hires. Real support.

By the end of the meeting, I was more convinced than ever. I understood why we passed on Fund I, but we needed to find a way into Fund II.

So I stayed close to the COO. Light touch. Check-ins. Relationship-building.

And then came the email, and my decision to blow up protocol.

I knew what I was risking when I replied.

Andy had a habit of giving impromptu tutorials on everything from value investing to manager selection, whether you asked for them or not. He taught me most of what I knew about institutional investing, and I'm incredibly grateful.

However, he was also a self-described micromanager of the highest order, as many leaders of successful, but lean organizations are. Our office literally had six thermostats for our entire floor, all clustered next to his desk. Institutional power made literal.

I'd been warned: Make no decisions solo.

But the window was closing. If I waited for Monday's team meeting, they'd be back on a plane.

My old boss at Lincoln once told me, "Sometimes you have to decide whether to ask for permission or forgiveness. Just be sure you're ready to live with the consequences."

I hit send.

A few days later, Andy stopped by my office. As always, I stood when he entered. As always, he reminded me not to.

"You scheduled a meeting with them for tomorrow?" he asked.

"Yes. The timing was tight." I replied.

"Do you know what day tomorrow is?"

I blinked. "Wednesday?"

"It's Yom Kippur."

My stomach dropped so hard I could have called in sick for the rest of the week. I felt my face turning bright red, the involuntary tell I'd learned to live with any time I was cornered, frustrated, or just caught off guard. I had accidentally scheduled a venture pitch on the holiest day of the Jewish calendar, a day that Andy would typically spend with family.

Not just any meeting. One with two founders that Andy barely tolerated at this point.

I told Andy he could just skip it, and Jim and I would handle it. "If I don't show, it looks like a snub, and that reflects poorly on Princeton and me personally. I'll be there," he said, already stroking his beard again. "But this can't happen again."

He was right. I'd screwed up. I was unfairly forcing him to choose between an important moment with family and his work duties, and I felt awful about it. I was now glowing so red, I felt like I could feel the blood vessels in my face bursting in the moment.

Our office's main conference room was really a repurposed open space, converted from an old dentist's office. No doors. Microwave in the back. More green duct tape holding the carpet together because someone thought it matched. It didn't.

The table was enormous, but oddly shaped—wider in the middle, like someone had tried to make a rectangle more collaborative. The chairs were so old that the springs were loose—so loose they'd send our guests flying backward if they leaned back without warning.

There was also a seating protocol. Andy always took the center seat. MDs flanked him. Then principals. Then associates. One summer, an intern sat in Andy's spot by mistake. The correction was swift, public, and witnessed by the entire twenty-person team.

The VC founders arrived. The technical founder wore khakis and a button-down. It was the late 2000s. Patagonia vests and Allbirds weren't the VC uniform yet.

When we were ready to get started, the VC's deck wouldn't load. Our old AV system, which required manual driver updates, seemed to have failed us once again. Our IT guy, a kind older man, fiddled with cables. The technical founder got up and started troubleshooting.

"You must know computers," the IT guy said. A few of us tried to stifle a chuckle. He had no idea who the VC was.

The VC who literally changed the world with his tech was standing there elbow-deep in our VGA cables.

The rest of us did what any good endowment team would do: held our breath, avoided eye contact, and prayed Andy didn't make one of his famous jokes.

Once things got rolling, they walked us through the Fund II plan. They'd made adjustments: fewer companies, bigger checks, deeper support. The platform wasn't a theory anymore; it was staffed and functioning.

From my vantage point in Andy's seating-chart pecking order, I had a good view of Andy, Jim, and other senior team members physically leaning in. The energy shifted. They weren't just tolerating the meeting; they were interested.

We walked them to the elevator. After they left, Andy turned to us. "Well?"

"That was impressive," Jim said. Coming from him, given the history, that meant a lot.

They offered us a small allocation—probably one of the smallest commitments we'd made at the time.

It might not have looked like much on paper, but it carried real weight. By Fund II, they were likely two or three times oversubscribed and able to pick and choose their investors. This wasn't about the dollars; it was about being invited into a scarce, curated LP roster.

Saying yes signaled humility—that we were willing to start small, prove ourselves, and earn a bigger place over time.

That modest amount was about getting back in the game.

And it worked.

By Fund III, we were all in: a much bigger allocation, tied as one of their largest investors. Over time, we would make it one of the endowment's largest relationships, across all asset classes.

The returns were outstanding. The platform became the model others copied.

But it wasn't always comfortable. One of the GP's social media presence was... active.

"Does he have to post so much?" Andy asked after a particularly loud thread.

"He's always been this way," I said. "As he says, he has strong opinions, loosely held."

"I just wish he thought about how it reflects on us. I guarantee I'm going to hear about this from a board member before the weekend."

It was a fair point. But that same boldness, his refusal to be boring, is what made him who he was.

What Compounds

Sometimes the most important decisions are made by people who don't yet have formal authority, but who do have judgment and just enough credibility to spend wisely. Leading from the middle means understanding the difference between institutional process and institutional purpose. Process exists to protect organizations from poor decisions, but it can also stand in the way of necessary ones. The key is knowing when careful deliberation serves the institution's interests and when speed matters more than consensus.

That recognition comes from being a student of organizational behavior, not just investing. Everyone's hesitation usually has logic behind it. Jim's skepticism reflected genuine pattern recognition from years of VC experience. Andy's extreme micro-management protected an institution where the small decisions mattered. Understanding those perspectives made it possible to distinguish between informed caution and institutional inertia.

Credibility to make that distinction comes from repeatedly demonstrating that you understand the stakes. When you advocate for something unconventional, it can't be because you're eager or optimistic. It has to be because you've done the work to understand why others are hesitant and still believe the opportunity warrants consideration. Conviction without preparation is just opinion.

Staying engaged with that firm wasn't based on a gut feeling. It was based on diligently tracking how they were executing their plan. When the moment came to reply to that email, the decision felt quick, but it represented months of relationship-building and diligence.

What compounds over time isn't just financial returns; it's trust, credibility, and the institutional permission to act on informed confidence. The immediate impact of our initial investment was modest. But compounding accumulated quietly before becoming visible. The relationship with the VC firm expanded beyond a single, small fund commitment into a long-term partnership that influenced how we approached similar opportunities.

More significantly, it changed our internal dynamics. Successful unconventional decisions built equity that I could spend on future unconventional decisions. Each time I demonstrated sound judgment on something non-obvious, colleagues paid closer attention to my next non-obvious recommendation. Senior colleagues started to encourage relationship-building with managers who weren't yet ready for our capital but showed promise. This created a valuable feedback loop. I earned more freedom to explore ideas before they became consensus positions.

We repeated this pattern many times over the years. We became more comfortable making small, early commitments to teams and strategies we found compelling, trusting that strong partnerships would deepen as we found ways to scale together. Perhaps most importantly, the experience taught me about the difference between taking smart risks and taking unnecessary ones. The decision to re-engage was based on continuing due diligence and relationship management. That distinction became crucial for every significant recommendation that followed.

What Endures

Years later, reflecting on that period, I'm struck by how ordinary the moment felt compared to its eventual significance. The conference room with duct-taped carpet, the AV system that wouldn't cooperate, the scheduling mishap that still makes me cringe. None of it suggested we were in the middle of something that would matter long-term. But that's how compounding works.

At my final Princo board meeting before leaving Princeton, Andy noted the impact of my pushing for us to take another look at this VC firm. He noted that sometimes a junior or mid-level team member in the room sees something that others miss, and that encouraging that perspective—even when it disrupts preferred processes—is how institutions stay ahead of consensus.

Career-defining moments rarely announce themselves. They arrive disguised as routine choices, an email reply, a meeting request, or a decision between following protocol and following an informed view.

Over time, I learned to trust prepared conviction over institutional comfort. I developed more confidence in making unpopular recommendations and the discipline to do the diligence that makes them credible.

The best decisions compound financially as well as strategically and relationally. They create opportunities that might be hard to envision when you make them.

The setting may be imperfect. The process may be flawed. But sometimes that's exactly how important things happen—in converted dentist offices with people who care enough about getting it right that they'll show up even when the timing is terrible.

CHAPTER 8

Drawing the Line: When Partnership Means Saying No

A T 5:05 P.M. ON a Friday, we were ready to hit send.

The timing was intentional. It was just late enough that no one on the other side would respond that day, but early enough to ensure they'd have to spend the weekend thinking about it. If they wanted to avoid escalation by 9:00 a.m. Monday, they'd need to work for it.

Our message was clear: We believed that the PE firm—different from the one in the earlier case—had proposed a coercive and unfair structure. Unless we were convinced otherwise by Monday morning, we were prepared to take things to the next level.

We didn't want conflict. We wanted fairness. But we also wanted them to feel pressure. Pressure often reveals what people are really willing to do.

Of course, no one pushes things this far unless they're either a) desperate or b) really, really confident.

We were a little of both.

The manager's proposal was a GP-led secondary, which was rare at that time in the early 2010s. There was no real playbook, just improvisation dressed up as innovation. Or in this case, coercion. The firm was clearly struggling to raise its next fund, forcing it to get "creative" with its terms to stay in business. The proposed structure required any LP who wanted to exit the fund with cash to vote in favor of amendments that would change the economic terms of the fund for everyone. Even those staying. So if you exited, you were required to hurt the economics of your fellow remaining LPs. And if you stayed, you got punished by the terms being weakened. Our estimate was that the large majority of LPs would exit, which would constitute enough votes to worsen the terms for those staying—all of whom would vote against the changes, of course.

It was like being told: You can leave the restaurant, but only if you throw your drink in the faces of the people at the table next to you.

It created a false choice: Take what we believed to be a below-market price or stay in and accept worse economic terms. Either way, someone got penalized.

The GP argued it was technically allowed under the fund's governing documents. That perhaps was true under a strict reading. But technical doesn't mean fair. And fairness, not syntax, is what fiduciary duty is built on.

To us, the structure didn't just feel wrong. It felt dangerous. If this became the new norm, every GP with a liquidity crunch could coerce terms under the cover of creative structuring.

We weren't going to be the ones who nodded that through.

As things turned around following the global financial crisis and Andy grew more comfortable with his and our success, our office finally got its desperately needed renovation, complete with glass walls, soft seating, and a modern open kitchen that we called the "cafe." But for those few weeks, our conference room situated off the main "trading floor" felt like a bunker. It was mostly me and Andy, weighing options, working the phones, trying to decide if we were really going to do this.

One morning during this period, Andy rolled in around 10 a.m., looking like someone who'd wrestled with his conscience all night and lost. The situation was clearly weighing on him. His shirt was slightly rumpled, and, as usual, he clutched a steaming cup of black coffee like it was the only thing keeping him upright. He didn't rush in. He simply arrived slowly and observed.

We brought in two expensive law firms: our usual New York firm and a Delaware specialist. The Delaware attorney was the kind of lawyer who'd argued in front of the Chancery Court more times than I'd been through TSA checkpoints. He wasn't cheap, but this wasn't a time to cut corners.

We also brought in university leadership—an extremely rare event. The president, a constitutional law scholar, asked a question I'll never forget: "What's their best argument?"

Not ours. Theirs.

I said, "They'll argue that LPs are sophisticated investors who understood what they were signing when they committed to the fund. That the governing documents we all signed allow it. That no one is being forced. We all have a choice."

"And your response?"

"Sophisticated doesn't mean powerless. And just because it's potentially *technically* allowed doesn't make it right. It's a breach of fiduciary duty."

The chair of our board was focused on something simpler: "If we sell, is the price fair? Tell me about the portfolio companies in the fund."

In PE, the GP marks or sets a value to each portfolio company in its funds at the end of each quarter. The sell price they offered in this transaction was meaningfully less than where they had just marked their portfolio last quarter. But the price wasn't the main problem, in our view. The structure was. We weren't just evaluating an exit. We were deciding whether to validate something that would undermine future governance in every fund like it.

At the advisory board meeting—a meeting of the fund's top investors, plus the GP—I calmly walked through why I thought the structure was coercive. The GP countered by saying that they were just offering liquidity, bringing in new capital, and keeping the fund alive. "This is a win-win," he said.

Later, on a separate call with the GP, I asked if they would pay for independent legal counsel for the advisory board.

"No," he said flatly. "It'll just slow things down."

That refusal told me everything.

Friday, 4:30 p.m.: It was just the two of us in his office. Andy was behind his desk, coffee long gone cold, staring at his computer screen like it might offer him an escape route.

"I keep thinking about the other GPs," he said. "What happens when word gets out? And it will get out."

He wasn't wrong. The private equity world was small. News traveled fast. We'd spent decades building relationships based on partnership, not adversarial tactics. Indeed, over subsequent years, Andy would tell this story to GPs on occasion.

"Our managers will hear about this by Tuesday," he continued. "They'll all start wondering, 'Are these the LPs who fight when things don't go their way?'"

I could see him running through the mental Rolodex. Every fund we were in. Every GP we'd backed. Every relationship that might suddenly feel different.

"What if we're wrong?" he asked. "What if we move forward and then realize we misread the situation?"

"We're not wrong," I said. "And if we don't act, what does that say? That Princeton can be pushed around as long as you do it cleverly enough?"

He leaned back in his chair. Stroked his beard.

"Decades of being the good guys. The true partners, not the adversaries."

"We're still the good guys," I said. "That's exactly why we have to do this."

He stared out the window for a long moment. The town and campus were quiet.

Finally, he picked up his phone.

"Do it," he said to our counsel.

As the lawyer confirmed he was ready to proceed, I turned to Andy and said, "This is the best we're going to feel about this. It'll get worse from here."

He didn't disagree.

Even while this professional standoff was unfolding, real life kept going. That weekend, Liz and I listed the money pit (aka our house) for sale. We had decided to move to a more walkable location in town. I spent Saturday driving around Princeton with the kids while showings happened. They were in the back seat, eating Goldfish crackers and playing on their Nintendo DSs. I was on and off the phone with our lawyers and bankers, trying not to lose my mind.

I was mid-call with the banker who'd helped structure the deal for the GP. Slick to the extreme. His tone was friendlier than usual, but still firm.

"You certainly got their attention," he said. "They're open to finding a middle ground. What's your bottom line?"

I knew what he was doing. Trying to get me to name a number. Give him something—anything—he could bring back to make the deal close.

I wasn't going to do it.

"We're sticking with our position. Status quo has to be an option. Anyone who wants to stay in the fund should be able to stay. Same terms. Again, it's what is fair."

He didn't love that. He launched into a new argument, talking over me, moving quickly... making the deal feel inevitable.

I needed a pause. Somewhere to think. And that's when I saw it.

A silver Lexus sedan, driven by a classic old-time Princetonian, was stuck in a snowbank in one of the university's surface lots. He had clearly tried to plow through a light berm the snowplow had left. Bad tires. Low clearance. Rear-wheel drive.

And, of course, it had a "Save the Planet" bumper sticker on it. Gas guzzler, virtue signaler... very on-brand for this town.

I told the banker I'd call him back in five, pulled over, and got out.

Gloves on, boots crunching in the snow, I leaned into the bumper. The driver, who was older and had surely been in town forever, never said a word. Just hit the gas while I pushed.

Eventually, the tires caught, the Lexus lurched out of the bank, and the guy drove off.

No wave. No thank you. Just gone. It didn't bother me, as I was starting to numb to behavior like that at this point.

Back in the car, my kids looked up and asked, "Why'd we stop?"

"Because he couldn't get out on his own."

I was starting to feel the same way at work.

Sunday night, 8:47 p.m.: The house was quiet. The kids were upstairs, the dishwasher was running, and I was back at the dining table with my laptop open and cold shepherd's pie still on my plate. Liz hadn't asked how things were going in a while. That was her way of showing support without adding pressure.

An email came in from our outside counsel. Subject line: "Progress."

Status quo would be offered. LPs who wanted to stay in the fund could do so on the original terms. No voting games, no forced consent to amended economics.

I called Andy.

"We got it."

"Got what?"

"Status quo. Original terms. For anyone who wants to stay."

He paused for a second. "So we don't have to move forward?"

"Nope."

"Good," he said. "Three gold stars for you—alright, see you tomorrow."

By Monday morning, it was over. Quietly, the line had held.

What Compounds

Partnership gets tested when interests diverge. For years, we'd built our reputation on being true partners with GPs—supporting them through tough times, giving feedback, and staying steady when others walked away. But partnership isn't just about being agreeable. Sometimes being a real partner means pushing back when something feels wrong.

That was what made the situation so hard. Princeton had worked with this PE team for years. Real partnership requires honesty, even when it's uncomfortable. When they refused to pay for independent legal counsel, that told me everything. They wanted LPs to act like partners when it suited them, but not when it cost them anything. True partnership means sharing decision-making, not just risk.

The hardest conversations often happen with people you respect. The strongest partnerships survive disagreement. We weren't trying to destroy the relationship—we were trying to save it by insisting on fairness. Any partnership—marriage, friendship, even an endowment team—gets stronger when you can disagree openly and still move forward together.

And, that's what compounded most: not performance, but trust. We built credibility, not because we were right, but because we were careful. We shared our reasoning, carried our costs, and refused to posture.

But I also learned that problems compound, especially when no one wants to address them. Bad deals compound into bad precedents. If we'd stayed quiet, that coercive framework might have become the template, copied by other GPs until LPs would be told, "This is just how these deals work now."

Silence compounds into acceptance. The GP was counting on institutional inertia—that we'd grumble privately but go along publicly. When you don't push back on unfairness, you're not just accepting it once. You're validating it for everyone who comes after. And, damaged trust multiplies across relationships. If word had gotten out that Princeton could be rolled by clever structuring, it wouldn't just affect this one fund. Every future negotiation would start from a position of weakness.

The market shifted. GPs began to include status quo options in future deals. But that likely only happened because someone pushed.

What Endures

Looking back, the market has evolved significantly since that moment. GP-led secondaries, often executed through continuation vehicles, have become widely accepted tools that balance interests. They give LPs the option for liquidity while allowing others to continue holding strong, long-term compounders. The best of today's structures generally work well and align incentives, providing flexibility without the coercion we once feared.

I recently had coffee with a partner from that same PE team, the one who'd been across the table from us through the whole ordeal. We met outside at a coffee shop in New York on one of my visits for an annual meeting.

He looked older, as I'm sure I did to him. His firm hadn't recovered after various challenges involving his boss, the founder. He said he was retiring now. His team was mostly gone. Everyone was looking for their next thing.

There was no apology. Of course, there didn't need to be. He hadn't broken any rules. But the machinery around him had collapsed, and now he was stepping off the field.

We didn't rehash the deal. But when I mentioned I was teaching now, taking a new path, he perked up.

"I have a friend who taught at the undergrad level after leaving the PE industry," he said. "I'll connect you."

It caught me off guard. He wasn't trying to smooth anything over. He was just... offering to help.

I found myself feeling something I hadn't expected: empathy.

He and I had both been shaped by the cultures our bosses created. Mine had built an environment of transparency, long-term thinking, and principled decision-making. His boss had created something different: something more aggressive, more transactional, less patient with process.

Neither of us had chosen those cultures. We'd both learned to navigate them as best we could.

Andy never would have proposed that coercive structure. Not because he was perfect, but because it went against everything he'd built his reputation on. But this guy? He'd been trying to execute his boss's vision while maintaining his own integrity. That's not an easy balance.

I could see him throughout our negotiations, pushing back where he could, softening edges when possible, trying to find at least a bit of middle ground. He wasn't the architect of the structure. He was trying to make it work for everyone, within the constraints he'd been given.

When you're second in command, you don't get to choose the strategy. You get to influence it, perhaps, but the driving force comes from the top. And from what I could tell, he'd tried to do that honorably.

A few weeks later, he emailed to say he was running the New York Marathon for charity, raising money for Memorial Sloan Kettering. It was something he now had time for.

We all try to find our way back to who we want to be.

I thought back to that snowy parking lot. The guy in the Lexus who never said thank you. Just drove off.

But maybe not everyone drives off. Maybe some circle back. Offer a small gesture of friendship.

You don't always get to choose the moment. But sometimes, the moment chooses you, and all you can do is lean in and push.

CHAPTER 9

Discipline in the Boom:
Backing the Builders

B Y 2013 AND 2014, the crisis was behind us. Private equity and venture capital were humming along nicely. Funds were growing in size, and companies were raising larger rounds. Multiples were expanding. Leverage was cheap and abundant. Almost everyone was making money and looking smart.

I recall our annual board meeting in Chancellor Green, an octagonal building on campus adorned with intricate woodwork and stained glass. The space, rich in history and architectural beauty, served as a striking backdrop to our discussions. This was one of my favorite Princeton traditions. Once a year, we would invite a professor to speak to the board about any topic, not necessarily investment-related. The board was there along with the university president, the provost, and the senior investment team, and we invited the entire Princo staff for the talk, followed by a reception. It was a way for the board to interact with the entire team, not just senior leadership.

On that particular day, in this nineteenth-century sanctuary of learning, we sat listening to one of the world's leading computer scientists explain a new technology that would potentially reshape finance: Bitcoin. The professor walked us through the cryptographic principles, the blockchain architecture, and the implications for monetary systems. You could see people leaning in, fascinated. This was likely the first time any of us had heard of Bitcoin and its technological breakthrough, and it was coming from one of the top computer scientists in the world.

Here we were, surrounded by stained glass and history, grappling with the most futuristic of technologies.

The reactions were immediate and mixed. Some were fascinated by the revolutionary potential. Others were skeptical: "Seems like a scam." "What is this supposed to mean for fiat currency?" At the reception afterward, the conversation shifted to deeper concerns. People were raising questions about the growing US debt and its long-term impact on the dollar. I was intrigued enough by the lecture that I bought some Bitcoin personally right after this meeting. It went up 10x over the next few years, at which point, I sold. If I'd continued to hold it until today, it would've been another 10x. Yes, another learning opportunity.

As we returned to discussing the broader investment environment, attendees expressed gratitude for how the endowment had recovered and how it was performing. But beneath the optimism sat a quiet, shared question: What happens when these good times inevitably end?

Strong markets create success stories that aren't always durable. Leverage amplifies returns, until it doesn't. Multiple expansion makes managers look brilliant, until prices stop rising. It's easy to mistake a rising tide for investing skill.

Inside our team, we focused even harder on where real value was being created.

The Bitcoin discussion crystallized something we'd been wrestling with across our PE and VC portfolio. In boom times, it becomes harder to distinguish between genuine innovation and momentum. Between managers who were building real value and those who were simply riding on favorable conditions.

In private equity, we leaned into managers who were true business builders: operators improving margins, driving organic and add-on growth, transforming operations. We avoided funds that relied primarily on financial engineering. When leverage is cheap and multiples are expanding, many show paper gains. But when more challenging times come, operational improvements endure and make companies more resilient.

In venture capital, we concentrated on early-stage managers who partnered with founders when companies were still being built, when VCs could genuinely impact strategy, help recruit talent, and open doors. We were cautious about late-stage venture. While there were some very talented managers who continued to add value at that stage, others were clearly riding momentum.

Each summer, when the new class of analysts arrived at Princo, we'd host a series of tutorials on the different asset classes. Jim and I usually took the lead on private equity and venture capital. It was held in one of those always-too-cold conference rooms with fluorescent lights humming and a long table full of eager, slightly nervous analysts with their notebooks open and pens poised, ready for insight.

Jim would start with our usual opener: "If there were an investable index for this asset class, like the S&P 500, but for PE and VC," he'd say, completely straight-faced, "we wouldn't invest in it."

In other words, if you could just buy into the average private equity or venture fund, it wouldn't be worth the risk. The only reason to play in this space is that you can be selective, backing the few managers who actually create value.

That line always landed with a thud, confusion, a few exchanged glances, and someone wondering, "Did he just say what I think he said?"

"Wait," one brave analyst would finally ask, "isn't it your whole job to invest in PE and VC?"

"Exactly," I'd say, walking to the whiteboard, grabbing a marker. "And that's why we're so picky." Then I'd proceed to draw a crude stick-figure face, meant to represent a founder or a CEO. The eyes would be mismatched, the smile lopsided, the hair just three lines straight up. Occasionally, I'd have him holding a laptop. It never helped.

"Look, I was never hired for my artistic talent," I'd say. "This is who matters. The people. The builders."

Then I'd scrawl a few key phrases: "Operational improvements," "Buy and build," "Incubation"—each one just barely legible. My handwriting is truly awful. I used to joke that my assistant could read it better than I could, which was both true and slightly terrifying. It had that classic lawyer's scrawl: rushed, overconfident, and completely indecipherable.

We'd talk through how, in private equity, we backed teams who were focused on improving operations—real business builders. Not just deal makers, but people who could take a strong leadership team and scale a company through thoughtful acquisitions and operational improvement. In venture, we focused on firms that partnered with founders from day zero. Some even incubated companies in their own offices. We wanted those who rolled up their sleeves, not just those riding the momentum of the market.

"These aren't Excel wizards trying to figure out how to maximize leverage," I'd say, tapping the board. "They're the ones out there building something real."

By the end of the hour, the whiteboard looked like the aftermath of a brainstorming session gone sideways: bad drawings, cryptic handwriting, half-erased phrases, arrows pointing to nowhere. But the message stuck. We weren't investing in trends. We were investing in people—people with vision, grit, and the ability to build something that could last.

It was messy, but it worked—because what we were really teaching was a mindset as much as finance.

We weren't trying to time liquidity cycles or predict when markets would turn. We were giving talented managers the space to build companies over many years.

What Compounds

The hardest time to focus on fundamentals is when fundamentals seem boring compared to whatever's working right now. In boom times, when everyone looks smart, it takes discipline to ask who's truly creating value and who's just benefiting from favorable conditions. The managers who survived multiple cycles were the ones focused on making their companies fundamentally better—not just more levered or more valuable on paper, but stronger at the core.

Curiosity and discipline, it turns out, aren't contradictory; they're complementary. It is important to be open to new ideas, even like Bitcoin. You must be curious enough to learn about innovations, while disciplined enough to distinguish between what's transformative and what's just trendy.

Building value in private markets—as we were doing at Princo— wasn't just about picking the right managers. It was about being the kind of long-term partner that value-building managers wanted to work with. That partnership, built on trust, shared standards, and long-term alignment, was what really sustained performance across cycles.

Over time, those lessons crystallized. Operational focus became a lasting competitive advantage. Companies that improved their fundamentals during good times were better positioned when conditions became more challenging. They had stronger teams, clearer strategy, and tighter execution.

Relationship depth grew into real trust. That trust allowed for more openness, more collaboration, and more willingness to be honest with each other when things weren't going perfectly, which, in investing, they rarely are.

Discipline sharpened judgment. The more we practiced distinguishing between luck and skill, between market tailwinds and managerial and leadership excellence, the more confident we became in our convictions. We stopped chasing what was hot and started doubling down on what was durable.

And conviction itself compounded into resilience. When you know the companies you're backing are led by real builders, you're less rattled by noise. You don't panic when the market hiccups. You stay grounded in what's real, what's being built, and what's going to last.

What Endures

Private markets became the compounding engine of Princeton's endowment, but only because we stayed focused on managers who were creating real value, not just paper gains.

That Bitcoin discussion in Chancellor Green still feels like a perfect illustration of a challenge many investors face. The world will keep throwing new ideas at you—some revolutionary, some momentary. The challenge is to stay open enough to notice what's real, and disciplined enough not to get swept away by hype.

The answer, I learned, is the same whether you're evaluating VC or PE managers: Focus on fundamentals, build for the long-term, and never mistake a rising tide for investing skill.

That mindset served us well across multiple cycles. And it still shapes how I invest today: Find the builders. The ones sketching out big ideas, sometimes literally, on whiteboards, who are determined to turn them into something real. Something that endures.

PART III

Compounding Relationships

W HEN WE TALK ABOUT compounding, our minds often leap first to numbers. Interest rates, investment returns, growth rates, data points neatly aligned in a spreadsheet. Yet the most meaningful compounding, in my experience, happens elsewhere: quietly, invisibly, in the spaces between people.

Trust, respect, camaraderie. These are slow, deliberate compounds. They build not from sweeping gestures, but from consistent, small acts of generosity, honesty, and genuine connection. They strengthen with time, patience, and shared experience. And, like the most enduring investments, the relationships that truly matter can yield extraordinary returns over decades.

One small habit I've always loved, perhaps even treasured, is raising a glass and saying "Cheers," or more often, the Irish "Sláinte." It's a simple thing. But it carries more weight than it seems. Whether it's with friends, family, or colleagues, that shared moment, glass to glass, eye to eye, is a quiet celebration of presence, connection, and intention. We're here. We made it. We're choosing to mark the moment together. This is such a habit to me that my kids warned their significant others (half-jokingly, half-seriously) not to take a sip until Dad makes a brief toast.

Over time, I've come to think of "Sláinte" as more than a toast. It's a philosophy. It means in Irish "to your health," yes—but also to your future, your path, your resilience. It's a reminder that meaningful relationships often begin with small, consistent gestures of respect and belonging.

Without relationships and community, all the compounding capital in the world means nothing. For me, one thing that often ties this part of my life together is faith.

You might have noticed that I was clearly raised Catholic in the Irish Riviera; that foundation has always stayed with me. But what has mattered most to me over the years isn't the denomination, but whether the preaching speaks to me. Since my twenties, I've most often worshipped at Episcopal churches, but for our Princeton years, I attended Nassau Presbyterian Church.

Besides its striking history—a 1766 Greek Revival landmark on the edge of campus once occupied by both American and British troops during the Revolution—what kept me coming back were Pastor Dave's sermons. They were deep, smart, and challenging in ways that stayed with me long after Sunday mornings.

One of my favorite conversation partners during my years in Princeton was a professor from the Princeton Theological Seminary, the father of one of my daughter's classmates. We'd talk regularly during coffee hour after Sunday worship, often standing in the corner chatting long after most people had gone. This friend was the best kind of conversationalist: a patient listener, thoughtful question-asker, and always full of gentle wisdom. After months of these chats at coffee hour, I finally asked what he taught at the seminary.

"Well, one of my areas is ministering to middle-aged men."

I burst out laughing; I thought he was joking, given the countless hours we'd already spent talking, with me unknowingly fulfilling the role of textbook case. But he didn't laugh. He was serious.

I said, "Wait...am I going to end up as a case study in your class?"

He gave me a small, mischievous smile and a slight chuckle, but didn't say a word.

At that moment, I was almost certain I already had.

In this section, we'll explore how relationships can shape one's career, but also one's understanding of life, leadership, and community. Because ultimately, the truest measure of a life isn't what we accumulate, but how we care for the relationships we nurture and sustain along the way.

CHAPTER 10

Who *Matters More Than* When: *Avoiding Calendar Math*

MARKETS WERE HEALING, AND with them, our willingness to look ahead again. As our confidence returned following the global financial crisis, we began to rebuild. This was after the long-overdue renovation, with new furniture, clean paint, and thankfully intact carpet. Though, in true university fashion, the HVAC system never quite worked right. The conference room was always freezing or overheated, and our ops team spent a decade—no exaggeration—arguing with the contractors about the system. (I'm certainly no HVAC expert, but perhaps it had something to do with having all the thermostats next to Andy's desk rather than in their respective zones.)

In one of those post-crisis private equity asset class meetings—everyone bundled up in Patagonia vests emblazoned with different VC brands—we found ourselves in a familiar allocator debate: commitment pacing. Several of our managers were back in the market and raising new funds in the same year, but we projected the next year would be light.

One of our analysts, eager and spreadsheet-fluent, looked up and asked, "Shouldn't we smooth our commitments? Stick to a steady annual pace?"

It was a reasonable question, and one that every allocator asks at some point. It seemed to come up at least annually, sometimes asked by analysts, sometimes by more senior team members, sometimes by board members who like neat charts.

It is *calendar math*, that institutional urge to smooth everything across years. It assumes talent is evenly distributed and timing is predictable. It looks good in Excel. It always sounds reasonable on paper. Consistent pacing looks disciplined. It satisfies models. It's easy to explain.

But it rarely survives contact with reality.

Managers don't raise capital based on our pacing models. The best ones raise when they see opportunity. When their current fund is mostly deployed. When their pipeline is strong. Not when it fits neatly into our fiscal year plan.

Trying to force smoothness would mean turning down strong managers just because several happen to be raising in the same year. Or worse, overcommitting in a light year just to hit a number, even when the options weren't compelling.

Early in my Princo tenure, we loosely used an annual budget for commitment. But eventually, we shifted. Instead of enforcing fixed pacing, we started using a rolling average over multiple years. It gave us some structure, but allowed flexibility to back managers we believed in when they were ready, and wait when they weren't.

We finally figured out that *who* you back matters much more than *when* they happen to be raising.

In investing (and in life), letting the calendar make your decisions is a good way to end up with neat-looking mediocrity.

The turning point came in 2013. Three venture managers we'd backed for years—each exceptional in their space—all came to market within a few months of one another.

If we'd followed our old pacing model, we might've picked one. Maybe two. But we backed all three.

We made the case internally: We'd pull forward commitments and go light the next year. But truthfully, we just didn't want to miss them. Not backing them felt riskier than overcommitting slightly. We felt that we were backing the right people at the right moment, regardless of what the spreadsheet said.

Ironically, while we were learning this in the portfolio, I was taking the opposite tack in my own career.

In my early forties, I started getting a lot of executive recruiter calls. CIO roles. Heads of PE. Some interesting, some serious, and some tempting—even two endowment CIO roles in Boston. Of course, I realize they weren't offers—just early feelers—but they were chances to get in the mix. I always said the same thing: Not yet.

I told myself I needed more time. More experience. A few more years in Princeton. I thought I was being prudent. And I assumed there'd be more calls. But they slowed. Gradually at first, then more noticeably. By the time I hit my late forties, the calls had tapered off dramatically.

After I moved to Boston, I got a call from a well-respected executive recruiter I'd known for years. I started pacing around my home office while we caught up. There was a pause in the conversation. Then, almost casually, he said, "You know, you probably should've made a move six or seven years ago."

I waited for him to laugh. He didn't. Then, after a moment, he said, "To be honest, it is important for you to be in your final role by fifty-five at the latest."

It wasn't exactly subtle. He didn't say why, but the implication was loud and clear: The industry and culture were shifting. I had said "not yet" a few too many times, and age had quietly entered the equation.

I hung up and stopped pacing, finally sinking into the sofa in my office next to my dog, Marcie. She was curled up, half asleep, and I rested my hand on her back as she sighed. For the first time, I wondered if I had mistaken patience for safety. I'd been so focused on proving I was ready that I hadn't stopped to ask what I actually wanted next—or what I was willing to risk to go after it. That realization stayed with me far longer than the recruiter's comment. It reframed the whole conversation in my mind; what had sounded like casual advice now felt more like a quiet verdict.

Reflecting on the call, I could practically hear the checklist in his head: Senior leadership experience? Check. Top endowment? Check. Strong track record? Check. Willing to relocate? Already did. Born after 1980?...Not so much.

Ironically, I felt more ready than ever. But readiness wasn't the only variable anymore. Our society is obsessed with youth, and I hadn't noticed how quickly that lens can shift. Saying "not yet" so many times was, in aggregate, a decision—a choice.

I started to see that calendar math problem everywhere. Students trying to optimize their résumés in perfectly-spaced intervals. Early-career professionals obsessing over the right sequencing of internships and jobs, so focused on assembling the "right" pattern that they sometimes forgot to ask important questions: What kind of work—and perhaps more importantly, what kind of people—would actually help them grow?

I'd try to reframe it for them: What if it's not about the timing? What if it's about *who* you're learning from? Work with great people. People who are invested in your future, who want to invest in you. Say yes to roles that stretch you, where you will have a great boss who wants to teach you. Look for cultures that value growth, not just achievement. Follow curiosity, not choreography.

Timing is convenient only in hindsight.

What Compounds

Not every decision can be reverse-engineered to look perfect on paper. Some of the best decisions come with lumpy pacing, uneven risk, and a high tolerance for uncertainty. If you wait for a clean window, you might miss the right door—whether that door is backing a manager, taking a job, or making a leap that doesn't quite line up with your plan.

Saying "not yet" too many times can harden into a habit—one that quietly becomes regret if you're not careful. My readiness wasn't a function of what the calendar said, but what my experience had taught me. Judgment matures through exposure and reflection, not just time served.

And often it matures more quickly when different generations are around the table. Colleagues who had lived through more cycles, who'd seen the gray between black and white, helped sharpen my own judgment. In today's culture, which often celebrates youth, I've found that the mix of lived wisdom and fresh energy makes teams stronger.

That lesson about judgment didn't just apply to my own path. It shaped how we invested, too. Relationships compound when we invest in them before we need anything in return. Our best partners emerge from relationships we build across cycles, through good markets and hard ones—connections that grow well beyond what can be captured in spreadsheets and pitch decks.

Trust builds slowly, but once established, it creates a foundation for candor and collaboration. Conviction compounds too. Every time we bet on people—rather than sticking to a pacing model—we become a little better at seeing what matters. We stop needing permission from the model. We start backing our own judgment.

And patience compounds into something more valuable than caution: It becomes judgment. We learn to wait—not for the perfect time, but for the right opportunity. To recognize that some moments are worth leaning in, others are worth sitting out, and that our job is to know the difference.

What Endures

That recruiter call still rings in my head sometimes. Not as regret, exactly. (After all, I still haven't reached his age cutoff!) More as a reminder. Of how easy it is to let timing dictate decisions. Of how tempting it is to believe there will always be another window.

I've come to see that waiting isn't neutral. In our portfolio, patience worked because it was active—rooted in conviction about who we wanted to back. In my own career, I've figured out that waiting without that same intention was a decision too—just one I wasn't consciously making.

We built a better investment process by letting go of calendar math and instead following conviction. We learned to back managers when we thought they were ready, not when it was convenient. We got better results. We built better relationships. We found our way to more exceptional outcomes by trusting people, not spreadsheets.

In the end, the calendar is a tool, not a compass.

Who matters more than *when*—whether you're investing in others, seizing an opportunity, or deciding it's finally time to invest in yourself.

Sometimes, I wish I'd backed myself a little sooner. Sometimes, I'm glad I didn't.

CHAPTER 11

Who *Matters More Than* What:
Investing in Friendship

I N THE EARLY SUMMER of 2020, I found myself doing something I hadn't done much before in my life: kayaking. It wasn't exactly planned. But then again, not much was that year.

My friend, Shahram, had the idea. "Perhaps we shouldn't be running next to each other right now," he said. "Too much huffing and puffing." This was still the early pandemic period, when people in Princeton took COVID very seriously, especially after the local nursing home outbreak hit the town hard.

"Have you ever kayaked?" he asked.

"Define kayak," I replied.

He showed up that evening with two kayaks strapped to the top of his SUV, a couple of life vests, and the confidence of someone who'd done this before. I'm not sure I'd held a paddle in a few years, but we shoved off into Lake Carnegie and started gliding (well, I flailed, he glided) past my colleague Jim's house, the tree line calm in the glassy water.

And that's how our pandemic routine began, kayaking two or three nights a week. Two friends. Two boats. One lake. Conversations that covered everything: work, family, university drama, the science of vaccine delivery, the mental fatigue of now working out of a windowless Zoom basement, and eventually, how I ended up investing in his company.

But let me back up.

Shahram and I met around 2017 in a local running group. Princeton isn't a big town, and eventually all the runners sort themselves into cliques of sorts: the serious racers, the slow long-distance folks, and the ones who run just so they can post about it. We were both solidly in the middle category.

We met on the usual loop through a bit of town and across campus. Introduced ourselves. He taught at the university. I worked at the endowment. We'd both done work in VC. And we both liked running.

Over time, we started meeting up for these weekly runs. Our conversation flowed easily from the VC world to families, the university, and politics. He had the kind of mind that could toggle from deep science to class structure to geopolitics to running shoes without breaking stride. And he was curious. Curious in that way that great educators and great entrepreneurs often are.

At one point, he mentioned he had only one female guest speaker in his VC course. And, when I looked her up, I noticed that she was a general counsel, not an investor. He acknowledged it, expressed frustration at the imbalance in the class and in the industry, and asked if I had any ideas. I introduced him to two of the best female VCs I knew. One of them ended up speaking in his class. It was a small thing, but it opened the door to more collaboration, more guest lectures, and more shared coffee runs.

I was grateful for the community that had brought us together in the first place—a loose band of runners who showed up week after week, rain or shine, bound less by pace than by the simple joy of moving together. The friendship grew naturally. Over miles run, guest lectures given, and increasingly deep conversations about work, mission, and what we wanted to do next.

By the time the pandemic hit, our lives had shifted. I was still at Princeton, but already starting to think about what came next. He was juggling his three roles and raising capital in one of the worst markets in recent memory. The kayaking wasn't just about staying fit. It became our way of staying sane.

We'd meet at Lake Carnegie around 6 or 7 p.m., shove off quietly, and paddle for an hour or more. It was calm. Peaceful. We talked about his company's progress, board dynamics, research data (some of which I understood), and our kids' remote schooling.

One night, we spotted something wiggling awkwardly in the water. It wasn't a fish, and it definitely wasn't a bird.

"Is that...a squirrel?" I asked.

We got closer. It was, in fact, a squirrel, doggy paddling across the lake with the wild-eyed determination of someone who regretted every life choice he had made to end up in open water.

"Did you know squirrels could swim?" I asked.

"I do now," Shahram said.

I don't remember what else we talked about that night. But I remember the squirrel.

———

After many months of this routine, Shahram and I hopped on our typical Tuesday night call. We were supposed to be going over his class syllabus. Shahram taught entrepreneurship at Princeton. He'd asked me to guest lecture in his course on venture capital and the finance of innovation, as I had done many times already. I'd show up, tell some stories about endowment management and partnership with VC managers, and leave the students mildly overwhelmed, but hopefully, intrigued.

"So, maybe we do the endowment investing overview first," Shahram said, "and then get into sourcing and due diligence of new managers?"

"Sure," I replied. "And, how are the other VC speakers shaping up?"

"All lined up! Although I feel awful for the students having to take these classes on Zoom."

It was our usual catch-up. I loved helping with the class. Shahram genuinely cared about the students learning something real, and it was very clear he cared about each of them as individuals.

In addition to teaching, Shahram was CEO and co-founder of an early-stage company. At the end of the call, I asked him how things were going with his startup, almost as an afterthought. He mentioned he was raising an angel round. I'd heard about the company for months on our kayaks: cutting-edge science that aimed to improve the delivery of biologic medicines, like vaccines. (Believe it or not, in addition to teaching and serving as CEO, Shahram was a partner of a VC firm. He had three careers, and somehow was amazing at all of them.)

I asked, "How's the round going?"

"Pretty good," he said. "Trying to build a little more runway, given the uncertainty in the world."

And then I asked a question that surprised both of us.

"Any chance I could get involved as an investor?"

There was a pause. "You'd want to invest?"

"If there's room. But only if it's not weird. No pressure."

He hesitated for just a second. I think he wanted to make sure the friendship didn't turn transactional. Later, on reflection, I think he was also worried about the pressure to perform when investing his friend's money.

"You sure?" he said. "I don't want you to feel like you have to. And I definitely don't want this to mess up our friendship in any way."

That's when I told him the truth: "I'd only invest if I were ready to lose it all. And I am."

After that Tuesday call, I did what I always did: I ran the investment past our chief compliance officer. Got the green light.

Still, I felt sheepish. I was a small check compared to most of the other angels. I didn't want Shahram to feel like he had to let me in just because we were friends. But when I told him I'd gotten approval and wanted to participate, his reaction was pure gratitude.

"Welcome aboard," he said. "I'm glad you're part of it. This is exciting!"

I filled out the subscription docs, wired the funds, and that was that. No beauty contest, no pitch decks, no endless diligence.

Just trust.

Later that summer, I told the analysts on my team that if anyone wanted a socially distant kayak hang, I'd supply the boat and the life vest. One of them, a brilliant but often late-arriving young guy, Hank, took me up on it immediately.

He showed up ten minutes late, saw me on the boat ramp with two kayaks, and sprinted full speed across the wet asphalt.

"Hey, careful, it's slipper—" I started.

Too late.

He hit the ramp, practically hydroplaned, and somehow managed not to wipe out. He landed right in front of me, breathing hard.

"I'm good! I'm good!" he panted.

Once he settled into the kayaking—and he was quite comfortable on the water as a former member of the university sailing club—we had a great conversation. He was thinking of grad school as a next chapter.

That moment, and many others like it, reminded me how even tiny, shared experiences can compound into something real. After grad school, he started a fund that invested in a concentrated portfolio of publicly traded companies, and I was very proudly one of his first investors. I continue to mentor him today and consider him a friend.

When the lake froze over that winter, Shahram and I started meeting outside around his solo stove. We'd talk science, life, and plans. Eventually, I told him something I hadn't told anyone besides my family, my boss, and my senior work colleagues: I was going to leave Princeton. It was a huge decision. He was happy for me. But visibly disappointed. I was moving away.

I would be back from time to time, as Andy convinced me to work "remotely" after moving, rather than my original plan of just cutting ties after our youngest graduated from high school. Fortunately or unfortunately, "remote" turned into a 300-mile commute, which was unsustainable. On the positive side, all that time back in Princeton did give me the chance to catch up regularly with my son for dinner, Shahram for Bent Spoon ice cream, and my good friend Mike for early morning runs on a regular basis.

Shahram and I continue to stay close. And I'm still kayaking, just now with my Aussiedoodle Marcie perched in the front of the boat like she owns it. I still text Shahram regularly with pictures of Marcie on the beach and in the kayak. And I'm still guest lecturing in Shahram's class at Princeton, but now also at Harvard Business School, Babson, and Boston University.

And I still feel like that investment bought me more than a cap table entry. It bought me a deeper seat in a friend's life's work.

What Compounds

Investing in a friend's dream is unlike anything else. It's not about chasing a return. It's about participating in someone's story. You get more updates, more emotion, and more pride when things go well.

You also feel more exposed. If it goes badly, you can't shrug it off like a write-down in a portfolio. The only way I knew how to handle that risk was to size the investment small enough that I could let go of the outcome while reminding myself that I wasn't investing in a result, I was investing in the relationship.

But in this case, I wasn't betting on a market or a molecule. I was betting on Shahram. I knew his story—coming alone to the US as a teenager, building a life here on his own, earning a PhD, becoming a Princeton professor, and building a company. I knew his character and how hard he worked. I knew he wasn't playing at entrepreneurship; he was all in. That's what made this so meaningful. It wasn't about strategy or timing. It was people-first investing in its purest form. Earlier, I wrote a chapter about how "who" matters more than "when." In this case, it wasn't just who over when. It was *who* mattering more than *what*.

That trust didn't appear out of nowhere. It had been compounding quietly for years—every mile we ran, every paddle stroke, every late-night call about new data and runway all added layers. And when the investment opportunity came along, saying yes wasn't a financial decision. It was the natural outcome of friendship—of showing up over and over again.

Curiosity compounded, too. The curiosity to ask, "How's the company going?" even if I didn't understand polymer nanoparticles. The curiosity to say yes to kayaking. To guest lecturing. To stepping into a friend's world. That curiosity became a habit, and eventually, part of who I was.

And honestly, it didn't hurt that one of the best VC firms in the world looked at the company and, though they passed (it was too early for them), they were genuinely excited about its potential. That outside validation meant something. But I would've backed him anyway.

I also realized something I hadn't before: My own "portfolio life" today—investing, advising, teaching—is in many ways modeled on Shahram's. He has three lanes: professor, startup CEO, venture partner. He's built a career not by choosing one track, but by committing to a few that reinforced each other. Watching him juggle it with energy and integrity has given me a blueprint I didn't even know I needed.

What Endures

Shahram's company is still early. Still building. But he's still excited. He still sends updates that occasionally go over my head, but always carry that same spark.

And we're still friends. I still guest lecture in his class. We still text. He still asks for pictures of my dog.

Perhaps the company will become a giant success. Maybe it won't. But that's not the point.

The point is: I get to be part of something real. Not just as a friend. Not just as a guest lecturer. But as someone who has believed in someone else's idea since before it was obvious. That's a rare feeling. And one I'm grateful to have.

Now, my dog and I kayak on the tidal river behind our house. And just this past summer, kayaking showed up in a different way—out in Cohasset Harbor with Jim, my former Princo colleague, and Pat, whom I first knew as a partner at one of our managers but who now counts as both a South Shore friend and my regular sailing partner.

Pat led us through the narrow channel into Little Harbor, a tidal basin you can only enter at the right moment with the tide. Inside, everything stilled. For nearly an hour, we floated peacefully, trading stories about old times—the camaraderie and returns we'd shared stewarding the endowment together, Jim and I as LPs and Pat as GP.

When the tide turned, the same current that had carried us in pulled us back out, this time into rougher water, where the outgoing tide met the incoming waves of the Atlantic. Jim and I were both in transition, having left institutional life, while Pat—steady, seasoned, quick to laugh even in tricky water—guided us through. The moment was a reminder: Currents may shift, but what matters is the friends paddling alongside you, and the ones who know the way through.

CHAPTER 12

The Partnership Flywheel: Learning Together Over Chicken Parm

"SO NOW *YOU'RE GOING* to do all the things you told *us* to do?" One of the co-founders of a newer VC firm—different than the ones I wrote about earlier—raised his Peroni as he said it, his voice warm and teasing. He's extremely tall, and the bottle looked silly in his hand, like he'd grabbed it from a dollhouse. The three of us laughed. We were at the back of an Italian restaurant in the Flatiron that they had rented out for their annual meeting dinner. The room was loud with LPs, team members, and old friends. Chicken parm was on the menu (my favorite), and the mood was celebratory. It was a couple of weeks before I'd be finishing up at Princeton's endowment on June 30, 2023, and it felt like a full-circle moment. Five years earlier, they were nervous first-time founders pitching in a WeWork. Now they were the seasoned ones. Now they were the ones hosting, guiding, leading... and I was the one moving on.

He was right. Now that I was about to leave Princeton's endowment and partner up with a former Princeton colleague on an investment firm, I was going to do all the things I had once advised them to do: to partner, to build, to scale. The irony wasn't lost on any of us.

There was something about sharing chicken parm that had always clarified things for me. Thirty-three years earlier, in a dorm room with a kitchenette, my friend Liz and her roommate had made the same dish for me and my roommate. During that dinner—perhaps it was the simplicity, maybe it was watching her care about getting it just right—I realized that I wanted her to be more than a friend. We started dating a few semesters later, and we've been married twenty-eight years now. Many of the best partnerships often start over the simplest meals.

I'd learned to trust what those honest moments revealed. Not the fancy dinners or carefully orchestrated meetings, but the times when people just showed up as themselves. When they made chicken parm instead of ordering sushi or some other fancy food.

It's a lesson I now share with my students: The most important insights often come from the simplest interactions.

But before that full-circle moment with the VC founders—five years earlier to be precise—I found myself in a very different setting, sitting across from those same two co-founders. They had started a new VC firm in a crowded WeWork in Manhattan. I had fortunately been introduced to them by the same COO with whom I had emailed many years before about the Yom Kippur meeting. It was one of my earliest experiences in the shared-office era, before the WeWork implosion. Glass offices lined the corridors, messy desks were visible through every glass wall, and startup energy hummed in the air. There was a communal area with coffee, snacks, water, and, surprisingly (happily), a beer tap. Muffled conversations leaked from behind glass-walled conference rooms and phone booths. I was there with Andy, our CIO, doing diligence on their emerging seed-stage VC firm.

It was unusual to meet a VC in a WeWork; venture capital firms usually had clean, modern offices meant to impress founders and LPs. I wasn't complaining, but even more unusual was how they'd laid out so many snacks: fresh fruit, cheese and crackers, nuts, and chocolate chip cookies. It was like they were just being themselves, which I loved. The snacks were humble, and they were clearly nervous, but something about them stood out. They were the type of co-founders you wanted to root for.

That night, we went to dinner across the street. Just the four of us: me, Andy, and the two co-founders. No fancy wine or sushi or tasting menu. PE and VC managers were often taking us out to sophisticated places, but I'm a much simpler guy—chicken parm, a burger, fish and chips, or shepherd's pie and a Guinness are more my speed. We went to a place that served solid, no-frills Italian-American food in a setting that didn't pretend to be more than it was. When chicken parm appeared on the menu, I knew we were in the right place. It felt honest.

On the train back to Princeton, Andy was quiet at first. Eventually, he said, "I'm not sure."

"I get it. There is a big balance sheet here, lots of pros and cons to committing," I replied. "Let's sleep on it and talk in the office tomorrow."

The next morning, back in Princeton, I made an unusual pitch. We stood on the "trading floor," our famously odd open floor plan. Desks in dog-bone-shaped pods, glass phone booths that weren't soundproof. Every "confidential" call was semi-public. Of course, it wasn't a trading floor, really more like a library. Andy's desk was positioned so he could see as many of the team members' screens as possible. The architecture of oversight.

He and I had debates that had become legendary in the office. Years earlier, when I was promoted to managing director, Andy said in his toast celebrating the achievement that I'd challenged him more than anyone on the team. I had no trouble speaking truth to power. The junior team members loved overhearing these exchanges. They'd literally take their AirPods out and lean in when they heard us getting into it.

My pitch wasn't just about returns. It was about learning.

"I think this duo has amazing potential. Their networks are deep, and they're leveraging data in a way that it hasn't been used in early-stage VC. They're innovating. (Over time, other VCs would copy their data approach, demonstrating they were onto something early.)

"However, they also have a lot of building and scaling ahead of them, and they've been incredibly responsive to our feedback so far. I think they can really help us grow our network, as they're connected to founders and emerging managers we currently don't know. We'll build something together. And in the process, we'll learn alongside them. We'll start small and scale as our confidence grows. I want to put serious time, energy, and attention into this partnership. This is the *partnership flywheel* we've been talking about; we learn together and hopefully win together."

Andy was stroking his face and beard. After many years, I knew this usually indicated annoyance or stress, but I also knew he often did that when I'd worn him down so much in an argument that he was about to give in.

We'd been developing the partnership flywheel concept for a while: that the best investments aren't just financial. They are relationships that compound, lessons that compound, networks that compound. As the partnership flywheel spins, we all get better. We help each other get better. Each revolution makes the next one stronger.

"Allocating is the liberal arts of investing," I added, repeating something I had heard Andy say previously. "We need to learn from different perspectives."

It worked. We committed. And over the next few years, I watched that theory become practice in ways I hadn't anticipated.

Fortunately for all, the firm grew into what we'd hoped it could become. They hired in operations, built out reporting, and transitioned from a duo in a WeWork into a real institution with a team, an office, and multiple VC funds. Not everything went perfectly, but their commitment to grow smartly never wavered. They kept building. Kept learning.

So did we.

At some point early on, we moved our communications from email and scheduled calls to a group chat with the two co-founders and me. It lowered the stakes for checking in. And, we could easily go from texting to chatting on the phone. It seemed like a small change in medium at the time, but it compounded into a closer, tighter relationship.

We tried to find opportunities for our junior team to learn from the experience, too, and I brought junior team members with me to meetings. I remember one session where an analyst peppered one of the co-founders with questions, and he walked through their sourcing process in detail, holding nothing back. We gave feedback, challenged decisions, and helped navigate tough calls. We weren't just advisors. We were learning, too. They opened our eyes to networks we hadn't seen, emerging managers outside our existing circles. Our network had been super tight-knit for decades. Suddenly, it had new nodes. The partnership flywheel spun both ways.

A few years later, early in the pandemic, summer 2020, my family and I rented a small place on Martha's Vineyard to escape the craziness in Princeton. No flights, just a ferry and fresh ocean air. The day we arrived was too beautiful to stay in the car. We stood on the deck, took our masks off, and breathed in.

I'd only been to Martha's Vineyard once before, back in junior high, when my friend Dave and I brought our bikes on the ferry with our town recreation department and stayed in a youth hostel. Let's just say I was hoping this rental would make for better accommodations.

The week before, I'd mentioned the trip on a Zoom call with the VC team. "We'll be there, too," one of the founders said. "Let's celebrate. Safely, of course, outside."

He came over with his wife. We greeted each other with elbow bumps—which was a thing for a brief time during the pandemic—

then sat on the patio, six feet apart but feeling closer than that. I recall we talked about life, family, politics, and the pandemic's impact on our kids. Afterward, my wife said, "They're so kind and inclusive. I couldn't believe they wanted to know what I thought, too."

That stuck with me. Real partnership extends beyond the conference room. It was one thing to understand that intellectually. It was another to feel it working.

What Compounds

Looking back, I realized what had made that partnership work: We grew together. Partnership starts before you need it. Those snacks in the WeWork, the honest dinner conversation, the willingness to be themselves instead of putting on a show—that's where real relationships begin. Not during the formal pitch or the contract negotiation, but in the moments when people just show up as who they are. Authentic moments reveal everything you need to know: chicken parm over sushi, a humble WeWork over a fancy office, iMessage over email, conversations that include everyone's voice over meetings that don't.

The best partnerships are learning partnerships. We weren't just investing in their fund. We were investing in their growth as managers, and they were investing in our growth as LPs. The partnership flywheel worked because both sides were committed to getting better together. That kind of mutual investment compounds in every direction.

Trust compounds when it's built through small, consistent actions rather than grand gestures—like the founders who remembered details about our lives, who followed up on casual conversations, who treated our junior team members with the same respect they showed us, who built trust that survived disagreements and difficult decisions.

Networks compound when partnerships are genuine. Because they respected our relationship, these founders introduced us to different managers, unique opportunities, and new ways of thinking. Our network didn't just grow; it got stronger, more connected, more valuable. Learning compounded too, because it flowed both ways. We taught them about institutional LP expectations, but they taught us about data-driven sourcing, emerging manager identification, and new ways to evaluate early-stage companies. Every conversation made both sides smarter.

Partnership requires showing up at different times—like the Martha's Vineyard visit during the pandemic, the late-night calls when there was a struggle or question, or the willingness to challenge each other when it would have been easier to just agree. That kind of commitment builds not just better business outcomes, but better people. Reputation compounds when you're known for being a true partner rather than just a check-writer. Other managers started approaching us differently because they'd heard we were willing to roll up our sleeves, provide real feedback, and invest time and attention in relationships. And joy compounds when work feels like a partnership rather than a transaction. Some of my best memories from Princeton aren't from the highest-returning investments. They're from the relationships where we built something together, where we cared about each other's success beyond the financial returns.

That's the power of the flywheel. Every genuine interaction, every show of trust and respect, every hard conversation and shared win nudges it forward. Over time, it spins with its own momentum, creating more trust, more learning, more opportunity. Eventually, the partnership isn't just a relationship—it's a perpetual force that makes everyone involved better.

What Endures

These days, post-Princeton, I'm working with VC firm founders, family offices, institutional investors, and students—building, advising, and teaching. That shift has given me a new perspective on what real partnership looks like, because now I'm the one asking for it as much as offering it. I think about these lessons on partnership constantly. And, in my work today, I try to be the kind of partner I valued when I was at Princeton. Someone who shows up authentically, who cares about learning together, who sees relationships as more than transactions.

I see too many professional relationships that exist purely for transactional reasons. People connect when they need something, engage when it's convenient, and disappear when the immediate purpose is served. Those relationships don't compound. They don't create lasting value. They certainly don't create joy.

The partnerships that matter—in investing, in career building, in life—are the ones where you genuinely care about the other person's success. Where you're willing to be vulnerable, to admit what you don't know, and to learn from people who might be younger or less experienced but see things differently.

That chicken parm dinner in the Flatiron, with the tall co-founder and his tiny Peroni, felt like the end of something. But it was really the beginning. Because the partnerships you build, the trust you earn, the learning you do together... those are the things that follow you wherever you go.

These days, when I'm evaluating whether to work with someone, I ask myself a simple question: Would I want to share chicken parm with this person? Not because I need them to like the same food I do, but because I want to work with people who value authentic moments over impressive presentations.

The best partnerships, like the best meals, are simple, honest, and nourishing. They fill you up in ways that go beyond the immediate purpose, and they leave you looking forward to the next time you'll share a table together.

Each meal, each conversation, each act of showing up is another turn of the flywheel. And over time, those turns compound into something larger than either side could build alone.

PART IV

Compounding Purpose

COMPOUNDING CHARACTER, CAPITAL, AND relationships are powerful, but their ultimate significance lies in service to something deeper: purpose. Purpose guides the trajectory of our lives, framing how we invest our time, resources, and energy. It defines what we accomplish and why we pursue it in the first place.

Over time, I've come to realize that true purpose often reveals itself subtly and quietly, emerging in moments of reflection, clarity, or even gentle humor. Yes, it's found in ambitious goals or professional achievements, but equally in simple joys, meaningful conversations, and the clarity gained from honest self-reflection.

For me, discovering purpose sometimes feels a lot like grocery shopping (at least the way I do it, which, to be fair, isn't very often). Between years of crazy travel schedules and Liz handling almost all of our household logistics, I probably went years without setting foot in a grocery store. But on those rare occasions when I do venture in, I walk in with the best intentions and somehow turn a ten-minute errand into a sixty-minute maze. I zigzag through every aisle three times, backtrack constantly, get distracted by seasonal displays I absolutely don't need (love Halloween candy time), and still forget the milk.

It's not that I don't try. I do make lists. I even started putting my list in order by store aisle so I wouldn't have to go up and down each aisle three times. It didn't help. When I get there, it's like I've never seen a grocery store before. The layout feels unknowable. The choices overwhelm. I walk miles to assemble a half-finished plan.

Purpose can feel like that. You think you know what you're doing, then realize you're wandering the aisles again. The key isn't getting it perfect; it's noticing the patterns. Learning your shortcuts. Being okay with forgetting the milk and trying again next time. What matters isn't the efficiency of the route. It's the persistence in showing up, paying attention, and adjusting as you go.

And purpose isn't just personal. Institutions, too, can embody purpose when they're built to serve as well as succeed. Take endowments, for instance: capital committed to values, managed with discipline, and sustained for generations. Whether in a university or a museum, that kind of purpose shows up not in a single moment, but across decades, even generations, of impact.

I've learned that purpose isn't static. It evolves as we do, growing clearer and richer over the course of a lifetime. Purpose reminds us to balance achievement with joy, seriousness with humor, and professional endeavors with personal fulfillment.

In this final section, we'll explore the quieter, deeper compounding—the kind that shapes legacy and enriches lives in ways spreadsheets never capture. Purpose gives meaning to all other forms of compounding, tying together the threads of character, capital, and relationships into a life that matters profoundly, authentically, and enduringly.

In the chapters that follow, purpose shows up in different forms: in the tension between markets and values, in the quiet lessons of the people who shaped me, and in the long arc of institutions built to serve generations. Taken together, they remind me that purpose isn't something we declare once; it's something we keep discovering, again and again, in the ways we live, invest, and serve.

CHAPTER 13

Invest Well to Do Good: Balancing Market Value and Your Values

A
S THE PRINCETON ENDOWMENT grew to a scale that drew more attention, a new kind of pressure emerged. Questions about purpose, responsibility, and impact became louder—sometimes from the outside, sometimes from within. And while those pressures felt institutional, they often landed personally.

For several of our years in Princeton, after we sold the money pit, our family lived in an apartment on Palmer Square. From our window, at a slight angle, we could see the Princeton Chapel perched on the highest point of campus. Despite being called a chapel, it was a vast, breathtaking Collegiate Gothic cathedral—one of the largest of its kind—able to seat nearly 2,000. Built from Pennsylvania sandstone, with soaring vaulted ceilings, intricate stained-glass windows, and a massive organ, it had a grandeur that felt more like a European cathedral than a college chapel. It was the scene for regular services of various faiths on campus, but also the start and end of the academic year: the Opening Exercises and Baccalaureate.

When the sun set in the evenings, the light would catch its west-facing windows, making the whole structure glow—like heaven was shining a spotlight on it. It was one of the most peaceful places on campus. Sometimes, during lunch, I'd go sit there and just think.

Our apartment was just a couple of blocks from campus, close enough that my walk to the office each morning felt more like a stroll through the neighborhood than a commute. It was also close to one of my favorite places in town, Halo Pub, a fantastic little farm-fresh ice cream and coffee shop. My routine was simple: stop at Halo for a coffee and a donut on my way to the office. I liked it because it felt unpretentious and familiar, the kind of place where I'd sometimes run into Rudy, the friendly maintenance man from Palmer Square, or William, our regular waiter at La Mezzaluna. Those small interactions made Princeton feel more like a community.

Amid this picture-perfect college town, Palmer Square felt like a postcard. Really, if you tried to imagine in your mind what the most classic college town looked like, Princeton would be it. The square had the post office on one end, a classic old building with this striking New-Deal-era mural that occasionally created some controversy over the way it depicted settlers and indigenous people.

That particular morning, my "commute" began as usual. There had just been a mini concert on the square over the weekend, so there were still a few remnants around, including a sign that read, "This is stolen Lenni Lenape land."

It was in this setting, surrounded by both Princeton's collegiate beauty and these reminders of more complicated histories, that I saw the flyer taped to a lamppost, calling out Princo directly for its investments in fossil fuels.

When I saw it, my immediate reaction was: "Hmm...that's interesting."

In our family, that phrase had a specific meaning. It was how my mom used to register disapproval without saying something negative. If she said your haircut was "interesting," it wasn't a compliment. So when I say it here, you can safely assume: I didn't love what I saw.

The language was pointed. We'd seen debates like this emerging nationally, including on our campus over the years, but seeing it plastered in my hometown square, interrupting my walk through this idyllic setting, felt personal in a new way.

Then came the rollercoaster in my mind that always happened when these things came up. First: *You've got to be kidding me.* Then: *These kids have no idea what they're talking about.* Then: *These kids are ungrateful.* Then: *Why are we doing all this work?* Then I'd think: *Hey, it's quite good that they're trying to make the world better, even if I think they'd be more effective directing their energy elsewhere.* And finally: *Hey, that's just part of the job of a university—to have these open discussions and debates.*

It was a jarring collision between my peaceful morning ritual and a public challenge to our work. But in hindsight, that tension was healthy: it forced me to articulate what we were really trying to do.

Inside the office, these conversations around outside pressures were becoming more frequent. Select students, alumni, faculty, and advocacy groups were calling for the university to divest from fossil fuels, and increasingly from other sectors and geographies as well.

These weren't easy debates. They rarely are. The core questions were challenging: What is the role of the endowment? Should the portfolio reflect moral judgments, and if so, whose? Should we use capital to take positions on social and political debates? How does the concept of intergenerational equity play into these discussions?

As we worked through these conversations, we kept returning to a principle that had always grounded our work: strong investment performance gives the university maximum flexibility to pursue its mission over time. The endowment existed to fund financial aid, faculty research, academic programs, new fields of study, and the intellectual life of the university across generations.

As the university would later state publicly, Princeton believed that its greatest contribution to improving the world's future would come not from reallocating the endowment's holdings, but through the scholarship, teaching, and research of its faculty and students.

Our role as investors wasn't to answer every political or moral debate directly inside the portfolio. It was to ensure that Princeton had the financial strength to serve its mission for generations. *Invest Well to Do Good.*

At first glance, it can sound like a contradiction—how can you both be disciplined about maximizing returns and claim to be investing ethically? I came to believe those weren't opposites but deeply connected tenets: Good investing demanded that we take values, risks, and long-term impact seriously, even as we kept performance as our central responsibility. We felt we could live "Invest Well to Do Good" by focusing on what we did best: generating the strongest possible returns that Princeton could then deploy toward educating students and supporting groundbreaking research.

Better investment performance directly translated into more research dollars that could be directed toward addressing the precise issues the protesters cared about: climate change, social justice, and environmental sustainability. Ironically, the stronger our fossil fuel investments performed, the more funding Princeton could provide for renewable energy research and climate science.

Our job wasn't to solve the world's problems through our portfolio positioning. Our job was to give Princeton the financial resources to do what universities do best: educate the next generation and fund research that advances human knowledge and addresses global challenges.

We partnered with managers who we knew were good, ethical people. These managers would naturally consider environmental, social, and governance risks in their investment process, not because of any ideological agenda, but because what serious investor would ignore material risks that could affect long-term performance?

The best managers we worked with understood that poor governance leads to bad decisions, that environmental regulations can reshape entire industries, and that social factors like employee relations and community trust can impact competitive positioning. They incorporated these considerations because it made them better investors, not because someone told them to.

We didn't need to impose environmental, social, and governance (ESG) criteria on our managers or exclude entire sectors from our portfolio. We just needed to work with people whose judgment we trusted, who thought comprehensively about risk and opportunity, and who could generate the strong returns that would give Princeton maximum flexibility to pursue its educational and research mission.

The principle was about excellence in the service of something larger than ourselves. To do what we did best—invest—so that Princeton could do what it did best—educate and research—in service of society's biggest challenges.

Princeton's informal motto is "In the Nation's Service and the Service of Humanity." It is inscribed in stone on the path in front of Nassau Hall. Whenever I walked across campus—walking my dog, heading to the chapel for quiet reflection, or on my way to lecture to a class—I'd see those words and think about why we were doing all this work. It was more than a motto. It was a quiet, constant reminder of what we were there to serve.

This approach never fully satisfied the most vocal advocates for divestment. They wanted immediate, complete separation from fossil fuel investments, regardless of financial consequences. Some saw any consideration of investment returns as morally compromised.

I understood their frustration. When you're confronting an existential threat like climate change, nuanced investment strategies can feel inadequate compared to the urgency of the challenge. But I'd come to believe that the binary choice, divest or don't, missed a more important opportunity. Princeton's endowment could accomplish more by funding the research that could actually address these challenges than by making symbolic gestures that might weaken our financial capacity.

The protests continued sporadically. Similar flyers appeared on other lampposts. But over time, some of the conversations evolved beyond simple divestment demands toward more productive discussions about how Princeton could most effectively address global challenges through both its investment strategy and its academic mission.

What Compounds

The most effective way to create a positive impact through institutional investing is to excel at investing first. Strong returns provide the foundation for everything else—scholarships that expand access, research funding that tackles global challenges, programs that translate academic insights into real-world solutions.

Trying to optimize for both financial returns and social impact simultaneously often leads to mediocrity in both areas. When you blur the lines between investment performance and impact goals, you make it much harder to measure progress in either dimension. It's much more effective to judge investment performance on its own merits, and then measure the university's impact through its research, teaching, and programs separately. That clarity of purpose allows you to excel at what you're supposed to do (generate strong returns) so that the institution can excel at what it's supposed to do (educate students and fund breakthrough research).

Values and performance don't have to be in conflict when you approach them with genuine sophistication. Some of our most successful investments were in companies and managers who were building solutions to pressing problems while generating competitive returns.

External pressure—even when uncomfortable—can force important conversations about institutional purpose and responsibility. The divestment advocates were asking legitimate questions about how Princeton's values should be reflected in its investment decisions, even when I disagreed with their proposed solutions.

Principled decision-making requires both conviction and humility. Conviction to stick with an approach you believe serves the institution's long-term interests, even when it generates criticism. Humility to keep questioning whether you're getting the balance right. "Invest Well to Do Good" extends far beyond endowment management. Whether you're building a career, choosing investments, or making any decision that involves both financial and values considerations, the principle of pursuing excellence in service of something larger than yourself creates more sustainable impact than choosing one or the other.

Over time, those principles compounded. At Princo, financial strength compounded into mission capacity. The stronger Princeton's endowment became, the more the university could invest in research addressing climate change, expand access through financial aid, and support innovative programs that wouldn't have been possible with constrained resources.

Integration of performance and purpose translated into better investment judgment. Understanding how environmental, social, and governance factors could affect long-term business performance made us more complete investors, not just more conscientious ones.

Institutional clarity deepened into more productive external relationships. When we could articulate clearly how our investment approach served Princeton's mission, we could engage more constructively with advocates, alumni, and other stakeholders, even when we disagreed about specific tactics.

Reputation spread among the managers we worked with. Investment managers respected our commitment to both strong performance and thoughtful consideration of broader impact, which led to better access to opportunities and more candid conversations about market conditions and investment prospects.

Purpose compounds into resilience during difficult periods. When market conditions were challenging or when we faced criticism for our approach, having clarity about how our work served something larger than financial returns helped maintain perspective and discipline.

What Endures

Years later, working with other institutions, I continue to encounter the same fundamental tension between financial objectives and values-driven considerations. The specific issues change—climate change, social justice, geopolitical concerns—but the underlying challenge remains constant.

How do you invest in a way that generates strong financial returns while also creating a positive impact? How do you balance fiduciary responsibility with social responsibility? How do you serve a long-term mission while responding to immediate community concerns?

The answer, I believe, is still "Invest Well to Do Good." Not as a slogan that papers over difficult tradeoffs, but as a genuine commitment to excellence in both investing and impact creation.

This approach requires discipline, sophistication, and constant learning. It's easier to choose one extreme or the other—pure profit maximization or impact-focused investing that ignores returns. But the integration of both objectives, done thoughtfully and rigorously, can create outcomes that are more powerful than either approach alone.

In a world facing complex challenges that require massive capital to address, we need investors who understand that building wealth and building a better world aren't conflicting objectives—they're complementary ones, when pursued with the right framework and the right intentions.

That flyer on the lamppost in Palmer Square forced me to think more deeply about these questions than I might have otherwise. Sometimes the most valuable lessons come from people who disagree with you, asking questions that make you examine your assumptions and clarify your principles.

Each semester when I'm back on campus to guest lecture, I find myself revisiting both the simple and the profound parts of that old life. I still get coffee and a donut from Halo Pub, and I still sometimes sit in the university chapel where I found peace during both joyful and difficult moments. Those rituals remind me that wrestling with hard questions, even ones posted on lampposts that disrupt a morning routine, is part of building something worth defending.

In those lectures, it's almost guaranteed that there will be one student in the back who raises his or her hand with a bit of a scowl to ask about ESG and divestment. I give an answer that aligns with what I learned from that flyer: That our job was to invest well so Princeton could do good. What always surprises me is that they don't push back, and that usually ends the conversation. Perhaps it's the self-selection into a class on venture capital, or perhaps after sharing so much of my personal history with them, they see me as a decent person trying to do the right thing. Or perhaps, just perhaps, I've made them rethink the issue.

Even when you maintain your convictions, the process of defending and refining them makes you better at what you do and clearer about why it matters.

CHAPTER 14

Persistence, Steadiness, Courage, Presence: Finding Purpose in the People Who Shape Us

IT WAS LATE AFTERNOON, and the window on the third floor of our house was cracked open. It was one of those late-summer days on the South Shore where the air sat around seventy-five degrees, the water was still cold because Massachusetts Bay is stubborn like that, and the tidal river looked completely flat. The sun and marsh air came in—salt, sun-warmed grass—that smell that meant the tide was working. I could hear seagulls arguing with each other somewhere overhead.

I had my music on shuffle. You could say my taste in music is eclectic. There is no real theme at all. Irish folk, then Bruce Springsteen, then Miley Cyrus, then R.E.M., then Rihanna, and occasionally hip-hop that samples older songs. This last genre is one of my favorites—when new artists take pieces of songs I grew up with and make something different out of them. That day, Pitbull's "Powerful Women" came on, and Dolly Parton's voice cut through, talking about family and work, and the beat made it sound both familiar and completely new. That combination of old and new layered together reminds me why I love the idea of compounding—one thing building on another and becoming something richer.

As I was listening to Pitbull's and Dolly's lyrics together, my mind went to an invisible thread running through this book—to the women who did more than their share and made it look normal. The four who keep showing up in my writing: my mom, my Nana, my sister Kristen, and my wife Liz.

Each of these women taught me something essential—persistence, steadiness, courage, presence—the heart of why I do what I do. Without them, there is no long arc of purpose. They didn't just shape the kind of people I seek out—loyal friends, curious students, trusted colleagues, and innovative managers—they shaped the reasons I choose to connect at all, and the kind of work I believe is worth compounding.

My mind moved back to my trusted coworker, my Aussiedoodle Marcie. She was sleeping under my desk, but if I moved an inch out of my chair, she'd pop up in two seconds, tail going crazy. I let this thought about four powerful women linger for a moment. I thought I'd paddle first, then come back and write. The board is where I do some of my best thinking.

Living on the marsh means you live by the tide schedule. You don't have to check it—you just know it. I grabbed the board, the paddle, and my life vest. Marcie was practically hopping with joy, ready for an adventure. Doggie life jacket first, then the leash. She knows how this works: no running out to the marsh until I say "Okay."

We walked out of the backyard down to the water. It was the best kind of day for paddling: no wind, warm enough that your hands wouldn't go numb, late enough in the day that the sun had started angling toward Boston. From where we were, if the sky decided to put on a show, it would throw colors northwest toward the city, and we'd get some free entertainment.

Marcie watched the marsh grass, waiting for permission. I lifted the paddle, listened to the gulls for a second, and took one good breath of this place. Then I pointed to the marsh and said, "Okay." She took off—full speed into the grass, running around in wide circles. After thirty seconds of pure joy, I got the board positioned in the water. Marcie jumped onto the front of the board, sat up like a figurehead, tail hanging into the water. We pushed off.

The first ten strokes are always mental noise—emails I forgot to send, some meeting next week I'll probably overprepare for, an article I half-read earlier. Then the water settles me down, the board finds its rhythm, and my brain shifts gears. That day, the thoughts came like the tide: my mom, my Nana, my sister, my wife. Four names I didn't choose together as a theme in this writing—they chose me.

My mom did the best she could with three kids, plenty of chaos, and, later, a second husband who most often created additional challenges instead of helping. Still, some things slipped through the cracks. We probably went too long between doctor visits. The school nurse sent home the same note about my eyesight every year, but it wasn't until fifth grade that I finally saw an eye doctor, and by then, I couldn't see the chalkboard at all.

The glasses helped immediately, and I wore them throughout middle school. But the summer before starting high school, I told my mom I wanted contacts. I told her it was because I wanted to join the cross-country team, and I didn't want to rock sports goggles.

But if I'm honest, I wanted contacts more for the faint hope that a certain girl might consider going with me to the fall homecoming dance. And the good news is, she said yes. Whether the contacts mattered or not, I'll never know—but they gave me the confidence to ask, and at least I could see her clearly on the dance floor.

At the eye doctor, they moved me through the system: eye exam, then over to the little teaching area on the eyeglass floor, where they taught me to put the contacts in with the help of a technician. The tech there was named Maureen. Of course she was—this is the South Shore, the Irish Riviera. Brown hair, blue eyes, fair skin, and a smile that kept showing up even when I was being hopeless. She wore contacts herself and told me so. I kept trying to see them in her eyes, which didn't help when I was also trying to get my own in.

My hands shook. I'd touch my fingertip to my eyelid, blink, and miss completely. Blink harder, miss again. The solution dripped everywhere, my eyes watered, and every time I messed up, it got harder to try again. Fifteen minutes turned into thirty. I kept glancing at Maureen, hoping to impress her somehow, which wasn't working. Finally, I gave up.

"I'm done," I told my mom. "I can't do it."

She didn't lecture me. She didn't try to fix it right then. My mom just put her hand on my arm and said, "Let's take a break, go home. And come back tomorrow."

I didn't want to go back the next day. She made me anyway. Same room, same mirror, same fluorescent lights. Same Maureen—still patient, still rooting for me. And somehow, that second day, I got one lens in. Then the other.

The world completely changed. There's a huge difference between seeing through something and just seeing clearly. I looked up at Maureen and could now see her face clearly—she was quite pretty, and her smile got even bigger when I finally succeeded. It was like someone had turned the focus knob on a camera. One second, she was just "the nice tech helping me fail," and the next, she looked like the cover of Irish American Monthly—flawless fair skin with just enough freckles to make it real, bright blue eyes, and that smile.

Getting contacts sounds like a small thing. It wasn't. When I started school, I joined the cross-country team. I started going to school dances. I started raising my hand in class more. Confidence compounds. It builds on tiny things: that second trip to Pearle Vision, a hand on my arm, a supportive tech named Maureen.

Out on the paddleboard, a small wave made the nose wobble. I switched the paddle to my other side and dug deeper.

Persistence looks dramatic in motivational speeches. In real life, it's more like switching sides with the paddle for the hundredth time until you find your balance again.

During two college summers, I interned at the John F. Kennedy Presidential Library in Dorchester. It's a striking landmark—a bold, white-and-glass building on Columbia Point, designed by I.M. Pei, with sweeping views of the harbor and Boston skyline that feel like a beacon of light and hope. I felt so fortunate to intern there. At lunchtime, I'd climb into my old car—broken air conditioning, vents that just blew hot air—and put the windows down so I wouldn't sweat through my shirt. Back in that period, I had R.E.M. in the tape deck most of the time. I had about five minutes to listen to the lyrics of one of my R.E.M. favorites. Then I'd turn onto my Nana's street, shut off the music, and shift into a completely different gear.

She always met me at the door. "Hi Teddy!" Like I'd been gone for months instead of one day. The house was spotless in a way that said someone cared about details. Not fancy—just looked after. She had the first floor of a two-family house; the kitchen was at the back with a window that looked out toward the expressway and the water beyond.

Before I could sit down, I'd see lunch waiting on the table: two tuna fish sandwiches on soft white bread, crusts cut off perfectly, sitting next to the window. A cold Sprite, beaded with condensation. A small pile of chips on a plate with a thin gold rim around the edge—a little bit of ceremony on a simple table. I never said anything, but I recall wondering if she prepared the sandwiches that way because that's how my dad liked them.

Out the window, I could see the Southeast Expressway looking like it always did: cars slowly moving through traffic. Well beyond that, Dorchester Bay opened up with Thompson Island in the middle distance, Spectacle Island farther out. I grew up hearing stories about Spectacle Island—that's where Boston used to dump and burn all its trash. By my second summer at the library, they were bringing dirt from the Big Dig construction project to cover up all that old mess.

Watching them build something new on top of something everyone wanted to forget felt like watching a kind of forgiveness happen.

To the left of the kitchen window, she had a washing machine right there in the kitchen—not hidden in a basement, just part of the room where it could hum along while WBZ 1030 played quietly on the radio, which was basically a steady loop of traffic complaints, weather complaints, and Red Sox complaints.

We'd sit and eat our sandwiches. She'd ask about my work at the library, whether they let me see anything really old and interesting. She'd ask if I had a girlfriend, and then before I could answer, she'd tell me I needed a haircut. I was hoping she didn't send me across the street and tell me to take my shirt off again, like when I was ten. She'd tell me about her most recent trip to Ireland to visit her cousin, Ida, in Dingle.

Those lunches taught me something I didn't have words for then: steadiness is its own way of showing love. You don't need big gestures if you show up in the same reliable way every time. Cut the crusts. Pour the Sprite. Ask the questions. Give the cookies. Send the person back out into the world feeling a little bit more solid about where they come from.

Decades later, my boss Andy, who knew the Kennedy family, brought me to their family compound on Cape Cod and introduced me to Ethel Kennedy, Robert Kennedy's widow and matriarch of the family. I told her my favorite part of interning at the Kennedy Library wasn't in the archives but in the lunches I shared with my Nana. She smiled, held my hand for the ten minutes we spoke, and offered beautiful words about the importance of family. She loved that the Library had given us that kind of time together.

Before the last turn of the river into Briggs Harbor and then Bassing Beach, the tidal river gets to its widest. Here, just before you enter the more open water, it gets really calm and flat. The marsh grass hardly moves.

People think steadiness is boring. They don't understand how powerful it is to know what to expect from someone.

When my sister Kristen finished high school, she went to George Washington University in Washington, DC, and built a real life there. She had close friends, including one of our favorite cousins, Megan. Kristen had weekend routines that had nothing to do with how we spent weekends on the South Shore. When I visited her as a high school senior, I saw something I couldn't describe then: someone designing her own days instead of just letting them happen.

When my turn came to apply to college, I kept it local and played it safe: UMass, Vermont, Boston University, Stonehill, University of New Hampshire, and Boston College. I got into all of them except BU, which is ironic because I now teach there. But, frankly, Boston College was what I wanted most—that was my dad's school and my real dream. When that acceptance letter came, I couldn't believe it. My grades were a rollercoaster, so I didn't expect to get in. At the time, I thought they were probably just being kind because of my dad's death.

Then, Stonehill complicated the decision. Because my uncle was a Holy Cross father, tuition was cut in half, plus they added an academic scholarship on top of that. Boston College, where I really wanted to go, would have meant taking on massive student loans. My dad's cousin warned me about the loans. "Graduate school is what matters later," he said. Maybe not perfect advice about choosing a school, but at that time, I felt he was right about debt. Of course, years later, I'd spend much of my career working on an endowment that was designed to make college more affordable for families with the same hopes and financial calculations. In truth, every one of my school choices—undergrad, grad school, law school—was driven by finances.

One of my life's proudest achievements is that Liz and I prioritized saving and investing over two decades, starting when I just finished school, so our kids could choose colleges freely. For me, that felt like compounding came full circle: Years of steady saving and investing turned into freedom of choice for them. But what makes me proudest isn't the impressive schools—it's who they've become along the way: curious, hardworking, resilient, and generous. That's the kind of compounding that matters most.

Putting aside money, in the end, Stonehill turned out to be exactly what I needed at that moment: a place to reset after high school, get my bearings, and prove to myself I could succeed in college. It was small enough that professors (several of whom were Holy Cross fathers) knew me, but demanding enough to push me. And the Holy Cross fathers were still looking out for me in ways that went beyond tuition help. In fact, Father Jim, who appeared early in this book and was a reliable presence at our family events, became one of my favorite professors of all time. He was one of the first people to ever get me to learn that writing can be therapeutic, centering, and clarifying.

It was a good year. But by the following spring, I could feel that pull toward something bigger. In May, our whole family drove down to Washington to watch Kristen graduate from GW.

May 10, 1992, was one of those rare, mild Washington, DC days. High of 73 degrees, no rain, with just enough breeze to move the flags around. The ceremony was on the Ellipse, with folding chairs set up for all the families. The White House was right behind us—so close it felt like President George H.W. Bush and First Lady Barbara Bush might be watching from a window. We could hear the city in the background: traffic on Constitution Avenue, sirens in the distance. There was that sweet cut-grass smell that every graduation ceremony seems to have.

Although it was a graduation, the setting stirred up a deep sense of patriotism and gratitude. I've told my kids many times that we're incredibly fortunate that my great-grandparents left Ireland to start anew here. Watching my sister graduate right in the center of the capital felt like standing inside a metaphor about American opportunity.

Samuel Skinner gave the keynote speech. He was President Bush's Chief of Staff. His words were inspiring. He talked about the "power of one"—how one good deed matters more than a bunch of good intentions, and I remember thinking we make courage more complicated than it needs to be. Maybe it's just looking for the next right, small thing to do and then doing it.

Later, we met Kristen's friends, saw her apartment, and ate at restaurants we didn't have back home. Walking back to my mom's car, I felt something that was half jealousy and half possibility. There was more to the world than what I knew. What exactly was I afraid of?

On the long drive back to the South Shore, we took turns picking the music. Visiting Kristen for graduation made me think of that R.E.M. song again, "Stand." I recall the lead singer describing it as being about making decisions, living your life, and not letting it just happen.

A few days after we got home, I called Kristen and told her what I was thinking. That I was impressed by what she'd built, that I wanted something bigger for myself, that I was a bit scared to try. She called GW admissions that same day, told them my story, and convinced them to look at my application, even though the window had closed months before. But Kristen did what Kristen does. If she wants someone to do something, she will convince them to do it. She will not give in. She doesn't get loud; she doesn't get angry. She will just keep making logical, thoughtful arguments until she convinces someone. She told me to apply right away. By the end of the month, I had an acceptance letter.

I transferred to GW that fall as a sophomore. That's where I met my wife. I got an internship with Congressman Studds. I studied International Affairs. My world got bigger almost immediately, and then it kept expanding. Kristen didn't just show me there was more out there. She gave me the phone number to dial and the confidence to call. And, I was so fortunate that she lived just a few blocks away while I attended GW.

———————————————

Out on the water, the wind shifted direction, and the board turned slightly. Marcie adjusted her weight without even thinking about it. That was something my sister taught me—how to change direction without making a big deal about it and still keep heading toward where you want to go.

———————————————

When we moved to Haddonfield, New Jersey—just five miles over the river from Philadelphia—so I could take the job at Lincoln Financial Group, I thought I'd finally figured out work–life balance. At the law firm, I'd been working eighty-hour weeks, seeing our kids at six in the morning (if I was lucky) and then maybe not again until the weekend—and even then, I usually had my laptop open. During that stretch, I had two assistants—one from nine to five and another from five to midnight—and most days worked alongside both. My new job felt like freedom.

I didn't know what to do with all that extra time, so I filled it with projects. I read the Philadelphia Inquirer every day like it was my job. I installed kitchen cabinets even though I had no business doing that type of work. I knocked out a wall that created a small closet in the kitchen, after getting a friendly contractor to assess it and promise the house wouldn't fall down. From the couch in the family room, I could see straight into the kitchen, where Liz would often be cooking.

One evening—pasta night—the water was boiling, and the sauce was simmering. Our kids were running around the house making noise, laughing, and throwing Webkinz stuffed animals around. I was on the couch with the newspaper spread out, reading headlines like they were going to change my life.

Liz glanced over from the stove, hesitating for a second, and said: "You've got this better work–life balance now. Maybe use a little bit more of it on the kids—I think they'd love that. They're looking for your attention."

I folded up the paper, wiped a kid's face, and joined the happy chaos in the room, quietly grateful to have a partner who could nudge me back toward what mattered most.

The next morning, I went for a run. Back then—and even now, when it is too cold to paddleboard or kayak—running was how I sorted things out. I got into a rhythm of breathing and footsteps. Somewhere between mile two and mile three, I reflected more on what Liz had said. I'd been given this gift of time, and I was wasting it on busywork instead of being present.

I'd been telling myself I didn't have a model for how to be a good father. During that run, I realized that wasn't an excuse. It was an opportunity. If nobody had handed me a template, I could create one myself. That conversation didn't turn me into Father of the Year overnight. It did something more important—it changed the question I asked myself. Instead of "Do I have time?", I started asking, "How do I use the time I have on the people that matter most?" This experience was one of the clearest reminders I've ever had of what true partnership can do—how the right person can help you become the version of yourself you most hope to be.

Out past the marsh, the tide started to turn. I always felt it in the board before I could see it in the water—a shift that started subtly and became a push. I pointed the nose back toward home.

The tidal river behind our house told the truth about timing. If you caught the tide right, you glided. If you missed it, you were fighting against the current. Today, we caught it perfectly. I kept a steady pace. Because most progress isn't fancy, it's just doing the same thing over and over until you get where you are going.

I looked back toward the northwest, toward the city, and Marcie and I were treated to one of those spectacular sunsets—the kind where the colors felt otherworldly. I recalled a sermon at Nassau Church in Princeton about "thin places"—moments in Celtic spirituality when the boundary between us and the divine felt especially narrow, where we got to sense God's presence more vividly. Living here in Scituate, our town on the South Shore, on the marsh, I've lost count of the sunsets where I've felt like that: heaven and earth just a few feet apart.

These four women didn't save me with big speeches. It was a second trip to Pearle Vision. Two tuna sandwiches with the crusts cut off. A phone call to admissions in June. A truth shared over pasta. Small actions, repeated, with love behind them. When I've fallen in the water—and I have—they're the ones who know how to pull me back up without making it about the rescue.

Marcie and I scraped up onto the marsh. I lifted the board out and unclipped Marcie's leash. "Okay," I told her, pointing to our house. I brought the board into the basement, cleaned Marcie up in the outdoor shower, and watched her settle into her favorite spot by the window where she could keep an eye on the neighborhood. The light was already different. The tide was going out.

I climbed the stairs back to the third floor. The marsh air was still coming through the window. I sat down at my desk.

Writing is just another kind of paddling—same motion, different element.

What Compounds

Persistence often happens in small rooms with fluorescent lighting and a friendly face across from you. At Pearle Vision, I needed someone to tell me to try again tomorrow and to believe I could do it even when I didn't. That moment turned into more than just getting contacts—it became the start of confidence compounding. One lens led to two. That led to joining cross-country instead of making excuses, which led to dances, which led to raising my hand in classes that once intimidated me.

Steadiness is its own kind of love. It cuts crusts off sandwiches, asks the same honest questions, and keeps the radio low enough that you can actually listen. Daily routines compound. Each small reliable thing stacks up until it becomes the kind of security you carry with you when you're far from home.

Courage sometimes comes from watching other people be brave first. I sat in the middle of Washington, DC, at a graduation ceremony with flags and clear weather and a speech about doing good deeds, and realized I could borrow my sister's courage long enough to build some of my own. A weekend in Washington opened up the map. Following my sister's path to GW started a chain reaction—meeting Liz, grad and law schools, a career that stretched me in ways I couldn't have imagined back on the South Shore.

Sometimes, the most meaningful guidance comes as a gentle nudge from someone who knows you best. Liz helped me see that time wasn't just something to manage—it was something to invest. Choosing to fold up the newspaper and get more involved changed the rhythm of my days. The more I practiced showing up, the more it felt like we were building our life in partnership—and the more rewarding it became.

Learning to listen also compounded over time. Nana's gentle questions made it easier for me to ask good questions later. Liz's honesty made it easier for me to take in what I needed to hear. My mom's patience—and Maureen's too—made it easier for me to be patient with other people learning difficult things.

Gratitude, perhaps most of all, has compounded. The older I get, the more I see that my better instincts are just echoes—borrowed steadiness, borrowed courage, borrowed ways of caring that these women showed me without trying to teach anything.

Skinner's reminder about deeds mattering more than intentions stuck with me. A few years ago, I started signing my emails "All the best" after reading President George H.W. Bush's book of the same name, not because it was clever but because it felt sincere. It's the tone I want my life to have.

What Endures

This book started with childhood because that's where I learned basic navigation. It comes back to these same names because you don't graduate from the people who shaped you. You just keep learning from them, even after some are gone. The facts haven't changed much between the different times of my life that I've written about. I have. That's what writing gave me when Father Jim made me try it at Stonehill, and again here, in this room with the marsh air coming in and a song about powerful women playing in the background.

And now, watching my own kids navigate their lives with strength and purpose, I can see that the foundation keeps building. It's like those songs I love that mix an old track with something fresh. The core is still there, but they've layered their own beat and lyrics on top. What my children are making now is entirely theirs, yet somehow it keeps shaping me too.

The endowment principles I've been writing about—patience, discipline, staying aligned with your values, thinking long-term—didn't start in investment portfolios. For me, they started in an eye doctor's office, a graduation lawn, and two kitchens.

When I get stuck on something, I still hear their voices.

From my mom: "We'll try again tomorrow."

From Nana: "Sit down and eat. Tell me what you're learning. And get a haircut."

From Kristen: "Pull the application out now. I'll stay on the phone while you do it."

From Liz: "Use your time on what matters most to you."

I don't think those voices ever stop. If I'm lucky, years from now, I'll be back in a quiet room, or out on the water with the sun angling toward Boston, thinking about and still learning from these same people. And if I'm very lucky, someone younger—perhaps one of my kids, or a Princeton, BU, or Stonehill student, or someone perhaps I'll never meet—will read this and recognize a piece of their own story.

For all of them, I hope they have powerful people in their lives—people who show up, tell them the truth, and help them see the world more clearly.

CHAPTER 15

The Long Arc of Purpose: How Endowments Compound Opportunity

W HEN I FIRST JOINED Princeton, about 8 percent of undergraduates were Pell Grant-eligible. (Students who are eligible are generally from lower-income households, so some use it as a proxy for the percent of low-income family students at the school.) By the time I left, it was 22 percent. Today, it is 25 percent. On a campus of 5,500 plus undergraduates, that's hundreds more students each year, students whose families may never have dreamed of a Princeton education.

That increase in access for low-income families wasn't magic. It was funded in large part by patient, disciplined stewardship, by an endowment structured not just to preserve wealth, but to expand opportunity. That ratio, 25 percent, represents thousands of lives altered. Generations lifted.

Each fall, I could see those numbers turn into faces as Liz and I attended the Pre-rade, a tradition for the first-year incoming class. (Not to be confused with the famous P-rade at Princeton reunions, which is loud and full of spectacle.) At the Pre-rade, first years march from Opening Exercises in the chapel, through the Pyne Hall Arch by Chancellor Green, and in through FitzRandolph Gate in front of Nassau Hall. Watching each year made it feel even more real, as we shared in the pride and purpose behind the work. It was always a great moment—seeing how excited and hopeful the students were, many of them the first in their families to be here. It became an annual reminder of why the work we were doing at Princo mattered so much to us.

And that's the part that compounds. When a student from a lower-income family earns a Princeton degree, the trajectory for his or her entire family shifts: for themselves, their siblings, their future children, grandkids, and even the communities they go on to serve. One life changes, and it creates the conditions for others to follow. The math of that kind of progress starts to look almost exponential.

Endowments are one of the clearest institutional expressions of compounding purpose. At their best, they grow capital in service of a mission—funding scholarships, research, community programs, and long-term institutional resilience. They require patient stewardship, with decisions made for the benefit of future generations rather than immediate gains. They are engines of progress, where today's investment decisions ripple decades forward, often in ways the original stewards will never see.

In all honesty, I didn't join Princeton because of the mission. I came for the people, the challenge, the track record, the quality of the work, and to learn from the best. I was drawn to the intellectual rigor and the culture of integrity on the team. The mission—the idea of stewarding capital to serve one of the world's great academic and research institutions—was abstract at first, almost background noise. But the mission found me. Over time, I came to feel its gravity—not loud, but steady. Sitting in meetings where our decisions translated into scholarships, faculty hires, or scientific breakthroughs gave the work a depth I hadn't anticipated. That experience shaped how I think about purpose today: not as a prerequisite for meaningful work, but often as its result. Sometimes, we come to believe in the mission by doing the work first and then seeing whom it serves.

At Princo, this integration of purpose and performance was embedded into the culture. In interviews and performance reviews, we evaluated analytical skill, curiosity, and teamwork, as well as a person's connection to the university and appreciation for the responsibility of stewarding its endowment. You could be brilliant on paper, but if you didn't respect the mission or grasp the gravity of managing capital on behalf of generations of students and scholars, you wouldn't be a fit. That mindset reinforced, day in and day out, that our work was not only technical but moral; a long-term act of service. And that sense of responsibility started with understanding where the capital came from in the first place. These were gifts, offered by donors who gave away their own wealth so others might learn, discover, and grow.

Seeing how rigor and purpose reinforced each other was one of the most powerful lessons of my career.

Working with endowments taught me that purpose and performance are not opposites; they're mutually beneficial. The best outcomes emerge when capital is managed in service of something enduring—when the *why* is clear, it guides every choice about the how. I came to respect the discipline required to think long-term in a short-term world. It's hard. The rewards are slow. But when you get it right, the impact is extraordinary. You fund discoveries that haven't yet been imagined. You support students who haven't yet been born. You provide stability through turbulent times. It's patient capital, aligned with patient ambition.

As Nobel laureate and longtime Princeton professor Val Fitch once said, "Excellence cannot be bought, but it must be paid for." That line has always stayed with me. Endowments don't guarantee excellence, but they create the conditions that allow it to flourish. They provide the foundation that allows institutions to take risks, pursue breakthroughs, and invest deeply in both access and achievement.

Princeton President Chris Eisgruber wrote in his 2025 State of the University letter, "An endowment is nothing like a savings account. It is more like a retirement annuity that must provide income every year for the remainder of the owner's life." Except that the owner, in this case, is perpetual. That framing captures the tension and responsibility of stewarding capital not just for today's needs, but for decades or even centuries. You're managing risk across market cycles, and even more importantly, across generations—always in service of a mission larger than yourself.

After reading President Eisgruber's letter, I sent him a quick note of appreciation. It felt important to acknowledge how clearly he articulated the stakes, and we had a brief exchange. These conversations about endowments may seem abstract to many, but they matter deeply. When people understand how thoughtfully this capital is managed, they're more likely to see its role in supporting institutions, as well as sustaining values, scholarship, access, and discovery.

In my final years at Princeton, I also served on the board of Princeton Presbyterians of the Westminster Foundation, a small nonprofit that supports their campus ministry. The dollars were modest, but the lessons were deep. The endowment was tiny compared to others I worked with, yet we treated it with the same care and intention. The foundation is led by two chaplains, Andrew and his wife Len, whose kindness, wisdom, and quiet strength made a deep impression on me. They ministered to the spiritual needs of students while also nurturing their emotional and personal growth during a formative time in their lives. At a university as intense and high-performing as Princeton, they offered a rare and needed refuge, a space where students could wrestle honestly with who they were and what they believed. Their ministry embodied the words they live by: *Do justice. Love kindness. Walk humbly.* Serving alongside them reminded me that purpose doesn't depend on scale. Even a small pool of capital deserves clarity, care, and alignment with the values it exists to serve. I've rarely seen a clearer example of what it looks like when purpose guides every choice.

Today, in the post-Princeton phase of my career, I continue to work with institutions that manage long-term capital, and I still feel that draw. Whether serving on investment committees or advising smaller endowments, I find purpose in helping organizations build the scaffolding for resilience and impact. It's not just about basis points. It's about what those basis points allow. I currently serve on the investment committee of the Museum of Science in Boston as a volunteer and as a member of the museum's board of advisors. That work, where the total dollars are much smaller than Princeton's, and helping to ensure the institution's long-term vitality, feels every bit as meaningful as anything I did at a larger scale. The museum's mission, to inspire a lifelong love of science in everyone, feels especially important today. In a world shaped increasingly by science and technology, public science education is vital for both kids and adults—for all. It's an honor to support that mission.

Gratitude, I've found, compounds into a deeper sense of purpose and meaning. As I reflect on all that endowments make possible, I feel a deep gratitude for those who built and sustained them. They wouldn't exist without the generosity of individuals who gave away their hard-earned money for something larger than themselves. Philanthropy is the root of it all. And alongside those donors are the people who manage these endowments—often passing up higher pay in private industry to serve a mission. And there are the board members who guide and support them. Over fifteen years, I was continually impressed by how dedicated and selfless many of these trustees were. Their primary focus was helping us do our jobs well, offering challenge, perspective, and encouragement, and showing what healthy governance looks like. Together, these stewards—donors, endowment managers, board members—are the reason endowments can thrive for generations.

If compounding character is about who you become, and compounding relationships is about whom you walk with, then compounding capital is about what you enable—and ultimately, the purpose you serve. Endowments, at their best, turn investment return into impact. Into opportunity. Into excellence. Into the flourishing of people and ideas that will outlast any one of us.

As President Eisgruber wrote, "The endowment leverages additional gifts... enabling Princeton to attract and support outstanding faculty members, move boldly into new areas of scholarship and research, and make its undergraduate and graduate programs affordable for every student we admit." That clarity of aligning capital with values transforms abstract mission statements into tangible outcomes.

And maybe that's the most powerful purpose of all: to put your energy, your discipline, and your judgment into something designed to serve others, long after your name is forgotten. To lay a foundation sturdy enough for others to build on. To trust that compounding, if rooted in purpose, can echo for generations.

What Compounds

Looking back, purpose isn't always clear at the start. It can grow slowly as you commit to the work and see whom it touches. Belief can follow action. I didn't arrive at Princeton looking for a mission; I found one by watching the impact of our decisions play out in real time.

Long-term capital demands long-term thinking, and that kind of thinking requires both imagination and humility. The most important results often take decades to become visible. Sometimes, the work is thankless in the moment but invaluable in the aggregate.

Of course, not every decision was perfect. Some investments didn't work out as we'd hoped, which is to be expected. More than a decade ago, one small co-investment even went to zero pretty quickly. We did a full post-mortem on it at an offsite, and talked about it regularly for years after. We did so, not to dwell on it, but to keep learning from it. And yet, reflecting on it now, that one small loss stuck with me more than many of the wins that generated billions of dollars in value. That's the strange gravity of failure: It lingers, even when it's just a blip in the bigger picture.

Looking back, I wonder if we gave enough space to celebrate successes or study what went right. To be fair, Andy often began tough conversations, especially at offsites, by asking what was going well and what we were proud of. That framing helped us recognize progress even when we were focused on what we could improve. The goal was never perfection; it was to keep refining judgment, iterating carefully, and staying committed to the long view.

Over time, I came to see that the most meaningful wins aren't always investments. Financial aid doesn't make headlines, but it changes lives—and those lives go on to change more lives. It compounds. It creates space for potential to be realized where it might otherwise lie dormant.

Each year of stewarding capital helped me better see the link between money and mission, and how to align them. With every decision, I gained a sharper understanding of what truly matters and what's merely noise. The responsibility of managing capital for others deepened my respect for thoughtful decision-making and patient growth. It was a quiet kind of leadership: slow, deliberate, essential. Watching real people benefit from abstract decisions reinforced my sense of privilege and accountability. The thank-yous from students I met when guest lecturing, the progress of funded research, the stability through crises—these were the dividends that meant the most.

What Endures

Endowments are expressions of trust—gifts from the past, stewarded in the present, to serve today and the future. There's something audacious about that—the idea that you can design something meant to last forever. For me, that sense of permanence is something I keep coming back to. In my faith, forever has always felt less like a promise and more like a calling—to live in a way that invests in what will outlast us. Endowments, in their own way, echo that invitation. They're built to endure and to serve; to create the conditions for others to flourish long after our own work is done. Stewardship—whether of capital or of faith—is about carrying something with care, so it can keep helping future generations when we're no longer the ones holding it. They serve purpose and continuity, built to outlast trends and weather storms.

Maybe that's why I've come to appreciate the name my mom and dad gave me: Edward, which means "guardian of wealth." When I was younger, I mostly thought of it as a source of confusion—why go by Ted if the name on every form was Edward? Only later did I come to see the fit. Almost too fitting, really, for someone who spent a career managing endowments. But the meaning goes deeper. To be a "guardian of wealth" isn't about possession; it's about stewardship— protecting resources so that others can benefit and grow. In that sense, my name has become less of a quirk and more of a reminder of the responsibility—and the purpose—I've been entrusted with. (Though

I'll admit, the connection between my name and occupation still comes in handy as a "fun fact" when I need one.)

If you're lucky enough to work with an endowment—or support one, or benefit from one—take a moment to appreciate the long arc of purpose it represents. It's capital, yes, but it's also conviction, carried forward.

And if you're managing your own portfolio, personal or professional, you could ask yourself first, what is this capital for? What will it enable? Whose future might it shape?

The most meaningful returns are measured in potential, multiplied over time, powered by purpose. For me, that purpose comes alive each semester when I return to campus to give a lecture on the allocator's role in venture capital. I talk with students about the partnership between investors and VCs, and how, when it's a true partnership, each side makes the other better. The students' enthusiasm always re-energizes me. Their questions, optimism, and seriousness of purpose remind me just how powerful these ideas are when they reach the next generation.

When I think about what endowments make possible, I picture those students at the Pre-rade—stepping through the gates into a future made possible by the work of countless people they'll never meet.

That sense of purpose has stayed with me well beyond my professional work.

Just a few years ago, during my mother's final hours, I was alone with her on a snowy night, at a nursing home on the South Shore. It was a

Sunday evening, and I knew that Andrew and Len, the chaplains who led the Princeton Presbyterians ministry, would soon be gathering with Princeton and Seminary students for Breaking Bread, their weekly worship service in Niles Chapel at Nassau Church. They knew about my mom, but I messaged them at that moment, as I sat by my mom's side. I let Andrew and Len know what was happening, that it was finally time. They responded immediately, with warmth and compassion. I took deep comfort knowing that in Princeton, 300 miles away from us, the small community I had helped support—these chaplains, and a group of Princeton students my work had helped reach—were praying for my mom and our family.

In a moment of deep grief and solitude, I felt surrounded by a community I had once served, and that, in turn, was now serving me. It was another reminder that purpose doesn't just echo forward. Sometimes, it circles back.

Conclusion *and an* Invitation

A few months after that office-hours conversation I described in this book's Introduction, the same freshman stopped by again. He hadn't slowed down much—still in more clubs than sensible, still racing forward as if he might miss something important.

But this time, he wasn't asking for advice. He was asking if I'd write him a recommendation for the honors program.

I said yes, of course. Partly because he was a good student, but mostly because he kept showing up to class, to office hours, to conversations about building a career.

He probably didn't follow most, or perhaps any, of the advice I gave him that first day. When you're that age, or perhaps any age, slowing down feels like giving up. Focusing feels like limiting your options. My advice might not have landed that day. But it might land later, when he's ready to hear it.

Writing this book has made me think a lot about timing. About the gap between when we start building something and when we realize what we've actually built.

And when I reflect on my own timing, I notice something else: At every turning point, I never felt fully ready.

Not when I decided to leave the law firm. Not when I cold-emailed Andy and Narv, asking the most respected investors in the world to give time to someone who had never allocated endowment capital. Not when I took on that messy secondary transaction nobody else wanted, learning as I went. Not when I started teaching freshmen who were definitely less nervous than I was. Not when my wife and I moved to the South Shore after what felt like a lifetime in Princeton, trading institutional prestige for something harder to explain at a cocktail party.

Not even when I sat down to write this book, wondering if anyone would care about the reflections of someone who'd spent most of his career on planes and in conference rooms, talking about other people's money.

In every case, I had doubts. Real ones. I second-guessed myself constantly. I still do. I wondered if I was qualified, if it was too soon, if I should wait until I had more experience or confidence or clarity about the outcome.

But I almost always moved forward anyway. Not because I was ready. Because I was ready enough. And I've come to believe that "ready enough" might be the only kind of ready we ever get for the things that matter.

And, I realize I'm not perfect at this either. I think back to that recent recruiter call at age 49—the one that made me realize I may have said "not yet" a few times too many—and I wonder what might have been different if I'd acted when I was only ready enough.

I've watched too many smart, capable people stall out waiting for perfect timing. Waiting for the next title, the next credential, the moment when the risk feels manageable. But that moment rarely comes. And while they wait for certainty, real opportunities pass by. Sometimes, entire careers pass by.

The people who build something meaningful—a portfolio, a company, a class to teach, a life with a spouse—share one trait: They act when they're ready *enough*. They understand the gap between ready enough and fully ready might never close. So, they move forward anyway and figure it out as they go.

That's what growth really is. Not being perfectly prepared, but being willing to step into problems you don't know how to solve yet, with people who might teach you what you didn't know you needed to learn.

This isn't about being reckless. It's about recognizing that preparation has diminishing returns. At some point, the next best thing you can do is start.

When I was managing Princeton's private equity portfolio, we used to talk about the risk of not having room for what was "coming down the pike." The concern was that investing in something today might crowd out something better tomorrow. You could build models forever and wait for perfect market conditions. Eventually, you had to decide. With incomplete information. Because perfect information doesn't exist.

Careers work the same way. Life works the same way.

That freshman understood this, even if he couldn't yet explain it. He wasn't joining every club because he had it all mapped out. He joined because he wanted to be in the room, around people doing things, in positions where he might learn what he was good at.

199

Was it scattered? Yes. Strategic? Not really. Was it better than waiting in his dorm room in Warren Towers for a fully formed plan to arrive? Absolutely.

Sometimes you must move toward something before you can see it clearly.

For all the lessons I've gathered from investing, teaching, and career transitions, the reminders that matter most often come from closer to home—like the times my kids made sure I stayed grounded. When they were in elementary school, we met my sister's family in DC on April Fools' weekend. We went to a Capitals hockey game at the Verizon Center, and during the third period, one of the kids asked to borrow my new iPhone. iPhones were fairly new at the time. I was distracted by the game, so I handed it over without thinking.

They gave it back a minute later, I put it in my pocket, and as we left the arena and started walking through Chinatown, I pulled out my phone and noticed something odd. Everything on my iPhone was in Chinese.

I looked around, confused. "This thing is amazing," I said. "It must know we're in Chinatown."

The kids nodded solemnly, playing along, acting impressed by my cutting-edge technology. It wasn't until we were back at the hotel in Foggy Bottom, and it was still in Chinese, and I was getting genuinely frustrated trying to navigate the menus, that they burst out laughing.

I tell that story not just because it still makes me laugh, but because it reminds me how important it is to stay grounded. No matter how fancy your title, how many meetings you're in, how many billions you and your team make for your endowment, you're never too far from being the guy who just got pranked by a third and fifth grader. And thank God for that.

After we moved to Boston's South Shore in 2021, I was still commuting back to Princeton—"working remotely" had somehow turned into a 300-mile commute. Most Mondays, I was up at 3 a.m. to be in the office by nine. One late night, I returned to our empty Princeton house and noticed something strange: The lights on timers were off. I walked room to room with my iPhone flashlight until, on the third floor, I found drywall scattered everywhere and a hole where an outlet had melted. In the basement, every breaker was tripped, and the panel was warped. I eventually pieced together that lightning had struck while we were in Massachusetts.

I texted Eugen—the same Romanian contractor who had helped us fix up our first Princeton house fifteen years earlier. He replied immediately. By 7 a.m., he was there with an electrician, calmly explaining what needed to be done. Then he offered me a ride to work in his truck. We talked about family, about moving on, and about never quite fitting in.

Eugen was one of the best people we met in Princeton—honest, fair, and deeply ethical. In a place where we often struggled to feel at home, he embodied a decency that reminded me why we were grateful to have landed there at all. Looking back, that night was a sign. After fifteen years and too many moves, we had never truly settled. The lightning strike just made it undeniable: That chapter was closing.

When I think back to that night when I was ten years old and our house caught fire, my sister pulled us through it. My mother, my Nana, my Aunts Re and Ann, Uncle Roger, our neighbors, teachers, the Holy Cross priests, and our friends—they got us through everything that came after. We didn't call it resilience. We just lived it.

That was my first exposure to compounding. I just didn't know what to call it yet.

Years later, I was offered a safe, steady job that made sense on paper. And then Line 2 rang. That call didn't change my life by itself. It mattered because of all the quiet forces that had been compounding: trust, preparation, reliability, perspective, steady care, small steps, hard work. Work that didn't show up on a résumé but turned out to matter a great deal.

And those quiet forces didn't come from nowhere. They came from people. From years of support, care, and belief. And the most enduring source of them in my life has been Liz. At every turn, while I chased the next challenge, we were building the life around it together—raising our kids, shaping our home, and holding on to what mattered most. She brought a steadiness that let me take risks, and I hope I brought the same for her. This book is about compounding, and our partnership is the clearest proof I know that small moments of support—offered day after day, year after year—can help build lives that are truly fulfilling.

At Princeton University, I saw another form of compounding—care translated into capital, and capital into opportunity. Small decisions inside the endowment office turned into real opportunities for people we'd never meet. Students who thought college was out of reach.

Researchers who needed time and freedom. The long-term thinking was more than smart—it was meaningful.

And years later, on that hike in Donegal, Ireland, when something guided me to sit on a bench to catch my breath. I didn't notice the plaque at first. But there it was: the name of Father Bartley, one of the priests who quietly helped our family after my dad died. I hadn't expected that moment. I couldn't have planned it. But in that moment, I felt the presence of everyone—and I mean everyone—who had ever shown up for us. I felt the force of their care. That's what compounding is. You don't always see it, but it will hold you up when you need it.

Writing this book has made me more aware of the subtle forces that have shaped my life. The decisions that didn't feel strategic at the time. The mentors who gave me time when they didn't have to. The bosses and colleagues who challenged me. The students who asked better questions than I was ready to answer. The setbacks that forced me to grow. The conversations that opened doors I didn't know existed. The phone calls that changed everything.

I didn't set out to build a life around compounding. But looking back, that's exactly what happened. One decision led to another. One relationship deepened into trust. Each lesson built on the last. This happens in all of our lives.

And not just with capital. Judgment, resilience, curiosity, and character all grow. So does the ability to listen longer, to ask better questions, to handle complexity without panic. These aren't things you learn from a book. They are things that shape not just how you work, but how you live, how you treat people, and how you understand what matters.

So, while I hope you have found value in these stories, I also hope you recognize that they are not a roadmap. I certainly didn't follow one. And they're definitely not a playbook, as every path is different.

They simply reflect a mindset.

A mindset that values depth over speed. A perspective that prizes relationships as long-term investments. An attitude that sees failure and setbacks as part of the journey, trusting that small, consistent efforts over time will build something meaningful.

And perhaps most importantly, the understanding that none of this is fixed. We're all still learning. Still making mistakes. After reading an early draft of this book, Liz pointed out to me the parallels between my BU freshman joining all the clubs and me taking on all these new roles after Princeton. Indeed, I'm still learning too. Still trying to build a life that grows in the direction of the values I believe in. Still trying to become a person worth compounding with.

If you're early in your career, you don't have to rush. But you also don't have to wait for perfect clarity. Ready enough is ready enough. The rest you'll figure out along the way.

If you're mid-career and worried you've fallen behind some imaginary timeline, you haven't. Some of the best investments happen later. Real compounding often looks subtle at first, like it's barely working—until suddenly it is, and the curve becomes exponential. Some of the most important growth only happens when you've stayed long enough to see a few cycles through.

And if you're leading others, whether you're managing capital, running a team, raising children, or teaching students, remember: Your example compounds far beyond what you can see. As my mother-in-law, Grammy, has often said to us, "You never know where you cast your shadow." People are watching how you handle setbacks, how you hold tension, how you balance confidence with humility. Those lessons travel farther than you think.

———

As I near the end of writing this, I've been thinking a lot about my mom. Before she was a stay-at-home parent, she had a short career as an English teacher. But even after she left the classroom, she never stopped teaching. I remember her helping my cousins, Matt, Joe, and John, and my friend Dave (all of whom appeared in this book) with their school essays. They'd bring her early drafts, and she read them carefully, offering comments, encouragement, a few edits in the margins. Matt mentioned it again recently when the extended family was all over for a barbecue—how kind it was, how much it meant.

I can't help but imagine handing her this book. I would have loved to get her feedback, not just as my mom, but as a teacher, a reader, and someone whose opinion always mattered. I can picture her reading it slowly, with care, and then gently telling me the chapter "Call Holding on Line 2" might have run a little long. I think she would've been proud. I'm sure she would have had some notes.

She wouldn't have used the word "compounding" to describe what she did—reading drafts, offering comments, and encouraging us. But that's what it was. Quiet support, repeated over time—shaping how we thought, how we wrote, how we would help our own kids... who we became.

The more I think about compounding, the more I'm struck by how countercultural the concept really is. It challenges both my instincts and yours, if you've come this far with me. We live in a world that appears to reward speed. That mistakes visibility for value. That teaches us to think in financial quarters, even in how we live. This book, and the life behind it, makes a quieter argument: that the best things grow slowly. And they grow deeply.

That's how endowments work. They don't chase headlines. They don't ride momentum. At their best, they invest with patience and purpose. They fund decades of progress, often without fanfare. Long-term engines of access, opportunity, education, and research. And most people don't even know how they work. Or worse, they make inaccurate, sometimes self-serving assumptions about them (yes, I know this sounds defensive, because maybe it is, a little).

We live in a moment when many of our systems feel brittle. Endowments, done well, don't just survive that pressure. They're built for it. Not because they're defensive. But because they're deliberate. They make decisions today for people they'll never meet. They don't follow the crowd. They follow the mission.

That mindset doesn't just belong in institutions. It belongs in how we live.

It belongs in the character we build. The capital we deploy. The relationships we nurture. The purpose we pursue. These are our personal endowments. They don't show up in Excel spreadsheets. But over time, they shape everything.

That's what endures. The rest, as always, is still compounding.

So here, at the end, I want to offer an invitation:

TO LIVE AND LEAD with the quiet conviction of an endowment.

TO INVEST in things that don't go viral, but last.

TO CHOOSE DEPTH in a world of distraction.

TO KEEP SHOWING UP—for your family, your friends, your work, your neighbors.

Because in the end, it's not just capital that compounds. It's character. It's relationships. It's purpose.

And when those things grow in the right direction—together—everything else can, too.

Afterword

The Identity Reinvention Project

When I finished my first draft of this book, I thought the story ended when I left Princeton and moved back to the South Shore. That was the arc I tried to capture. But in the months after my departure, I found myself writing an essay to process the transition—partly for myself, partly for my senior colleagues who left Princeton shortly after I did, and partly for anyone navigating a big career change later in life. It doesn't fit neatly into the book's narrative, but it follows the arc of my life, picking up where the book's story leaves off. I've chosen to include it here as an afterword, because what came next—the messy, humbling, and rewarding work of reinvention—feels like an important part of my journey too.

In the 1988 film *Funny Farm*, Chevy Chase plays Andy Farmer, a New York sportswriter who quits his job to move to rural Vermont and write the great American novel. The fantasy is perfect: pastoral setting, creative freedom, a simpler life focused on what really matters. Of course, everything goes spectacularly wrong. The locals are eccentric to say the least. The house is falling apart. The novel won't write itself. By the end, Andy is paying the townspeople to act normally so he can sell the house and escape.

I thought about Andy Farmer a lot after leaving Princeton's endowment in 2023. Not because my post-institutional life went wrong, although it certainly went differently than planned. But because I'd fallen for my own version of the fantasy. After fifteen years managing private equity and venture capital investments for one of the world's leading endowments, I was ready for the next chapter. I figured I'd move back to the South Shore of Massachusetts, where I'd grown up but hadn't lived since I went to college, and build a different kind of professional life: teaching, writing, investing, advisory work. Less institutional, more entrepreneurial. Less singular, more varied.

Like Andy Farmer, I had romanticized the transition. I was about to discover that you can leave the institutional world, but your institutional identity doesn't leave you quite so easily.

The first few months after leaving were liberating, disorienting, and restless all at once. After fifteen years of being "Princeton's PE guy," I was no longer defined by one institution, but I also wasn't quite sure how to describe what I was.

Here's something I've discovered about the players in the allocator world: Everyone is romanticizing everyone else's life.

Our PE and VC managers, I'm certain, imagined us living some kind of Ivy League fantasy. They probably pictured us reading poetry on the lawn in front of Nassau Hall, debating philosophy between investment committee meetings, strolling through Gothic arches while contemplating portfolio theory. The reality would have disappointed them: fluorescent-lit conference rooms with broken HVAC and endless revisions of Excel PE fund sizing models.

Meanwhile, we romanticized their lives. The carried interest riches. The private jets. The power to transform companies with a few board meetings and a new CEO. We conveniently forgot about the broken deals, the LP pressure, the brutal fundraising cycles, and the partners who got pushed out when returns lagged.

And all of us, allocators and managers alike, romanticized the ultimate escape: leaving it all behind for something "meaningful." Moving to the country. Writing the book. Teaching the next generation. Building something new. Living a life that seemed more authentic than conference rooms and carry calculations.

This mutual delusion kept us all going.

Princeton is a company town in the most traditional sense. When you worked for the university's endowment, you couldn't escape it. Every weekend trip for ice cream at The Bent Spoon, every dinner at Teresa's Restaurant, every run across campus, you'd run into someone from the university.

The town knew who we were. "Oh, you work at Princo," became a conversation starter and ender. People had opinions about what we should invest in, what we shouldn't, how we should think about fossil fuels, China, private prisons, or whatever the controversy of the month happened to be.

This visibility created a strange dynamic. I was never off duty. My professional identity followed me to coffee shops, the gym, our kids' school. I couldn't just be Ted. I was Ted from Princo, steward of the university's billions, target of everyone's investment opinions and moral judgments.

When I decided to leave, a small part of me was escaping this fishbowl existence. I imagined a life where I could just be myself, undefined by a single institutional affiliation. What I didn't realize was how much that constant definition had become part of my identity. You don't know how much you need the fishbowl until you're swimming in the ocean.

Leaving Princeton definitely wasn't retirement; it was my reinvention. I was 50, with hopefully decades of work ahead. The question wasn't whether to work, but how to work differently.

Within a year, I had:

- Joined an investment firm, partnering with a former Princeton colleague to invest in an endowment-inspired strategy
- Started teaching at Boston University (actual first-year undergrads)
- Continued guest lecturing at Harvard Business School and Princeton
- Joined several boards and investment committees
- Became a strategic advisor to two VC firms
- Started writing about investing, life, and teaching

- Joined a boat club (because apparently that's mandatory on the South Shore)
- Bought a Dodge Ram pickup truck (fulfilling a childhood dream)
- Bought a Porsche (for...less clear reasons)
- Started listening to country music
- Installed multiple Ring cameras around our new property
- Became obsessed with the wildlife they captured

If this sounds like someone frantically assembling a new professional identity from available parts, that's because it was. The simplicity of "I work at Princeton" had been replaced by a complex portfolio of activities that took a paragraph to explain.

The boat club seemed like a perfect South Shore move. Unlimited access to center-console boats to take into Massachusetts Bay and on the North River with no maintenance headaches, just pure enjoyment. What could go wrong?

Docking. Docking could go wrong.

After my first few attempts at bringing the boat back to the slip, attempts that involved creative profanity, dock hands running to fend off my approach, and entertained day drinkers watching from the deck at TKO Malley's Pub, I developed a system. I'd call the marina on my cell phone as I entered the harbor.

"This is Ted Karns. I'm about five minutes out. I have no idea what I'm doing. Seriously. Please have all hands on deck at the slip. I mean it. Everyone. It's going to be ugly."

They thought I was joking the first time, but soon they had a full crew waiting with boat hooks and patient smiles. "Don't worry, Mr. Karns. We've got you."

The mighty institutional allocator, who once confidently deployed hundreds of millions into the top private equity funds, couldn't dock a boat smoothly. The irony was too obvious to ignore.

Nothing prepares you for the ego adjustment of going from somebody to nobody. At Princeton, I'd grown accustomed to a certain level of professional privilege. The best managers in the world came to our offices. At meetings, people sought out our opinions. Our allocation decisions moved markets, or at least LP market participants.

The first manager annual meeting I attended post-Princeton was a masterclass in humility. In this world, seating charts aren't accidental. At annual meetings and dinners, where you sit signals how much influence you have. Being at the lead table means your voice—and your fund's capital—carries weight. I went from sitting at the head table to being just another small LP in a room full of small LPs. I wanted to say, "Don't you know who I used to be?" But of course, that was exactly the point. I used to be someone who mattered in their world. Now I was just another guy with a small LP commitment.

The operational adjustments were equally jarring. No more awesome IT guys to handle tech support (at Princo, we had the best IT team ever, by the way). No more assistant to manage my calendar (at Princo, I had the best executive assistant ever, by the way). I spent an entire afternoon trying to figure out how to integrate Zoom scheduling into my Outlook calendar.

Just when I was getting comfortable with my new status as "formerly important," the universe threw me a curveball.

One of Boston's most legendary investment firms invited me to their annual dinner. I assumed I was included out of courtesy, a nod to my past rather than my present. I prepared myself for placement at the equivalent of the kids' table by the kitchen.

Instead, I was seated at the lead table. To my left: the legendary firm founder, a value investor whose market calls moved billions. To my right: another legend, this one from the endowment world, with literally the most well-known PE fund sizing model in history.

I spent the entire dinner wondering if they knew I'd left Princeton. Was this a seating chart error? Did someone forget to update the list? Or was there some kind of institutional half-life where your former affiliation continued to emit reputational radiation for a period after departure?

The conversation was sophisticated, forward-looking, important. For three hours, I felt like my old professional self. Then the dinner ended, and I drove back to the South Shore in my Dodge Ram, listening to country music, wondering what in the world had just happened.

The physical move from Princeton to our new town of Scituate was only 300 miles. Culturally, though, it sometimes felt like I was Andy Farmer landing in Redbud, Vermont—a different world with its own rules, rhythms, and cast of characters. I felt a bit like a fish out of water.

Princeton: buttoned-up, achievement-obsessed, professionally curated. Every social interaction began with "What do you do?" followed by a subtle calculation of relative status. I once said hello to a woman walking her dog, and she responded, "Do I know you?" As if greeting strangers were a breach of social protocol.

Scituate and the South Shore: the Irish Riviera, where not saying hello to strangers is considered rude. And stopping by a neighbor's house to just chat feels natural. Also, apparently, day drinking is a thing here—my new neighbors introduced themselves by bringing over beer at 2 PM.

The safety culture was another adjustment. In Scituate, almost no one locked their doors. Most people leave their car keys in the cup holder when they park on Front Street in the harbor. I once mistakenly got into a car that looked just like mine, with keys in the cupholder, nearly starting it before realizing it wasn't my vehicle. In Princeton, you locked your car religiously. Car thefts were, unfortunately, a near-monthly occurrence.

Even summer fireworks felt different. In Princeton, fireworks meant Reunions weekend: fully permitted, every safety precaution taken, recycling bins everywhere, perfectly timed to the playing of Old Nassau. In Scituate, you headed to the beach and watched your neighbors shoot off professional-grade fireworks. Not sparklers, not bottle rockets, but serious explosives—launched by the guy from two streets over, holding a Bud Light can. It was both thrilling and mildly terrifying.

But here's what really struck me: I joined a local run club, the Waverunners, and it was revelatory. My fellow runners could not care less about my professional pedigree. No one asked where I worked. No one cared about my Princeton years. It was one of the most welcoming communities I've ever been part of—Liz and I have made some close, supportive friends there. We show up for each other—in running and in life.

The Ring cameras were supposed to be for security (I was still in Princeton mode when we moved in). They became wildlife cams—my new obsession and unexpected metaphor for transition.

Every morning, I'd check the overnight footage like I used to check the morning market news. Coyotes, foxes, deer, raccoons, possums, skunks—our South Shore backyard and marsh were apparently Grand Central Station for local wildlife.

One morning, a coyote stared directly into the camera for a full 30 seconds. I swear it was thinking, "What are you doing here, Princeton PE guy? Shouldn't you be at a manager meeting?"

Upon reflection, I realized that I've traded my institutional life for a portfolio life. A "portfolio life" is simply a career made up of multiple roles instead of one all-consuming institutional job. And here's the truth that no one tells you about it: A portfolio life is actually as demanding as institutional life, just in a different way.

At Princeton, I had one job with a massive scope. Now I have multiple roles, each with its own rhythms, requirements, and responsibilities. Teaching demands constant preparation and presence. Investment committee work requires deep dives into different organizations' challenges. Writing requires discipline and vulnerability.

But here's the thing: I'm not overwhelmed at all. I'm energized. Each role informs the others. Teaching makes me a better investor. Investing makes me a better IC member. Investment committee service makes me a better teacher. The variety that initially felt a bit chaotic has become symbiotic.

When I discuss career paths in finance with my students, I can now speak from experience about the realities of institutional life versus the romanticized versions we all carry, a perspective that only came through living both sides of the transition.

The families and nonprofits I work with aren't getting a distracted retiree. They're getting someone who is active in investing and bringing institutional experience to more focused engagements. Someone who can dedicate real time to their specific challenges.

When someone asks what I do now, I still struggle with the elevator pitch. But I've stopped apologizing for the complexity. "I invest, teach, advise, and serve on investment committees" might not have the punch of "I manage Princeton's PE portfolio," but it's honest and sustainable.

The country music started as a joke. Driving the Ram seemed to demand something different than my usual playlist. Within months, I was unironically singing along to songs about dirt roads, whiskey, and small-town life while driving to the ferry into Boston.

At some point, it dawned on me: I'm acting like I'm a city guy who moved to the country, but I'm literally from here. I'm acting like a fish out of water, but I grew up here.

But the music spoke to something about the transition, not from city to country (or fishing town, really), but from institutional to independent, from singular to plural, from defined to reinventing.

By year two, I'd found my rhythm. While the boat docking had improved marginally, I quickly learned that it is better to have a friend with a boat than your own boat. The Ram had found its purpose hauling kayaks and dirt for fixing the lawn's wet spots. The Porsche... well, some identity crisis purchases you just live with (and really enjoy).

The teaching had evolved from nerve-wracking to genuinely rewarding. The investment committee work feels substantive and impactful. Even the wildlife had become routine, although I still gave the coyotes respectful distance.

This wasn't the simple life I'd imagined. It was actually more complex than my Princeton years. But it was complex by choice, not by default. I'd traded the simplicity of institutional identity for the richness of a more varied professional life. That being said, I could certainly see myself going deep again (in yet another reinvention) for the right combination of best-in-class investing, combined with meaningful impact.

You don't realize how much your institutional identity defines you until you try to leave it behind. The transition isn't retirement; it's reinvention. You're not stopping work; you're reimagining it.

The fantasy of the simple life after institutional investing is just that: a fantasy. You don't become Andy Farmer in Vermont, finding pastoral perfection. You become Andy Farmer in the middle of the movie, dealing with unexpected challenges (like hostile wildlife), new skills to master (like boat docking), and a creative project that's harder than expected (like writing a book).

But here's what the movie doesn't show you: Eventually, you stop trying to be Andy Farmer at all. You stop romanticizing what you left behind and what lies ahead. You accept the messy middle ground of a life that's neither institutional glory nor pastoral simplicity.

You learn to answer "What do you do?" without cringing. You stop checking whether you're at the head table or the kids' table and just enjoy the conversation of those around you. You realize that the coyote staring into your camera isn't judging your life choices. You are.

And sometimes, on a perfect New England morning, when the marsh is at its prettiest, your students are engaged, and the investment committee meeting was productive, you realize that this is what you were actually looking for. Not a simpler life, but a more intentional one. Not retirement, but renewal.

The stories we tell about careers are often oversimplified—polished for cocktail hours or LinkedIn bios. In reality, they feel uncertain, nonlinear, and full of moments where you're asking yourself: Is this it? Learning to normalize and even be comfortable with that feeling early on is a true gift. Of course, it took me a little longer. But today, I'm more comfortable iterating, learning, being open to wherever the path might lead next, and refining it as I go.

The only difference between me and Andy Farmer? I'm keeping the house. This isn't escape. It's homecoming—three decades and an identity reinvention later.

Acknowledgements

THIS BOOK WOULD NOT exist without my wife, Liz. You've read draft after draft—dozens of them—and made it better every time. Like everything else in my life, you have been my partner in this, too. At one point, after yet another round of edits, you told me I should change the title from *A Compounding Life* to *Everything That's Ever Happened to Me* by Ted Karns. You weren't wrong. For decades, you have been my partner in every sense—the one I turn to first, the one whose perspective I trust most, and the one who steadies me when I lose my footing. When doubts crept in or the risks felt too great, you never wavered. While I was busy racking up miles to BOS, SFO, and LHR for Princo, you were the one keeping our home and our lives moving. If there is a better partnership in marriage, I've never seen it.

To Matthew and Julia: When each of you was born, I felt like God had blessed Liz and me more than we could have ever hoped for. My greatest pride is in who you are today: kind, principled, and independent people. You also lived this book alongside me—all of my quirks, the endless conversations around the table about the endowment model—a subject you knew so well by high school, you could have written this book yourselves—and the many old stories (probably told too often) about my chaotic childhood. My fondest memories from Princeton have nothing to do with work. They are the weekends the three of us spent riding bikes across campus, stopping for ice cream, and resting in Prospect Gardens. And as proud as I am of your journeys so far, I'm even more excited to see what lies ahead for you both.

To Kristen, my sister: You've always been a steady supporter in my life, and I'm deeply grateful for that. Your encouragement and thoughtful edits here made this book stronger, but even more, your care and loyalty have been constants I could always count on. Having an avid reader and librarian as a sister is unfairly lucky when writing a book—and having you as my sister is an even greater gift.

To my mother-in-law, Mary Louise (Grammy): In our family, you carry the voice of your generation—one that once included my mom and dad and father-in-law. You do it with such wisdom, humor, and steadiness, and I know they are looking down from heaven with pride and gratitude. I'm also deeply grateful for the support you've given Liz, Matthew, Julia, and me along the way.

To my friend Shahram: You inspired me to build a portfolio career, get into the classroom, and turn my essays into a book. You also made sure I got out on the kayak—and for that balance, I'm equally grateful. Without you, I probably wouldn't have done it.

To Ben, my publisher and editor: Thanks for guiding a clueless first-time author through the process. Your notes had a pattern: First, I resisted them, then I slept on them, then I admitted you had truly helpful suggestions. It turns out that it's a very effective editorial method. Your insights made the book far better, and I'm grateful. Thanks also to Marie for your careful eye in catching errors and tightening the prose, and to Caerus, whose thoughtful approach to the book's design shaped how the finished work comes to life on the page.

To my colleagues through the years: At Bingham, Lincoln, and Princo, and now at Boston University and Copperplate—the investment committee debates, the strategy sessions, and even the disagreements taught me more than any textbook ever could. I particularly want to thank Jim. For fifteen years, you were my partner in private equity and venture capital—thoughtful, steady, loyal, and relentless in your pursuit of better decisions. I couldn't have asked for a better colleague or a truer friend. And to the family offices, nonprofits, private equity, and venture firms I've had the privilege to work with: Your partnership and trust have been just as much a part of my education. I thank Princeton University—not just for the chance to do work I loved, but for shaping my sense of purpose through its informal motto, "In the Nation's Service and the Service of Humanity," which continues to guide me.

To my dog, Marcie, who reminds me daily that life is actually quite simple: Get outside, eat well, have some fun, take naps, and love the people we share our lives with, unconditionally.

To the many friends and family members who read drafts, asked probing questions, or simply listened as I worked through ideas—Liz, Matthew, Julia, Kristen, Andrew, Noah, Lauren, Jim, Tom, Becky, Jane, Andrew and Len, Shahram, Nelia, Hank, Peter, Jen, and Rachel:

Your curiosity and honest feedback helped me see my own story more clearly. I'm also thankful to those who read an essay or chapter along the way, offering thoughtful perspective, including Aaron, Nnamdi, Brad, Jim, Andy, Jenn, Theo, Jon, Pat, and Jeff. And to those who shared their own stories with me over the years, reminding me that everyone has a compelling journey worth sharing.

Gratitude, in the end, runs through all of this. I am grateful to live in the United States of America—and in the Commonwealth of Massachusetts, which I'm honored to call home—whose freedoms and opportunities, secured by those who have defended them, made this journey possible. Above all, I thank God for Liz, Matthew, and Julia (and for meeting me in my continuing doubts and drifting denominational loyalties), and for the constant reminder that what matters most is love, family, and community.

About the Author

TED KARNS IS AN investor, endowment manager, attorney, and educator. He spent fifteen years as a Managing Director at Princeton University's $34 billion endowment, where he co-led the private equity and venture capital program, supported the university's mission of funding scholarships and research, and mentored rising investors. He now advises family offices, nonprofits, and investment organizations on long-term strategy and governance, and teaches finance at Boston University. His work focuses on helping people and institutions think long term.

*While hiking in Donegal, Ireland, Ted stumbled upon this bench
dedicated to Father Bartley, the former president of Stonehill College
and an important figure in Ted's early life. This moment reminded Ted
that no matter where you are in life, your people are looking after you.*